Uncover Incredible Secrets!

You've just opened the door to a world full of wonder and the unknown. Your exclusive copy compiles over 2020 facts across 101 unique themes, covering everything from the mysterious dinosaurs to incredible culinary world records.

Immerse yourself in thrilling tales about deep-sea creatures, discover the unusual abilities of animals, and uncover the secrets of the human body. Each page of your new book is a step into an astonishing journey filled with discoveries and amazing truths.

Imagine unraveling the mysteries of black holes, exploring the histories of ancient civilizations, and laughing at the most amusing musical experiments. This book is your personal key to the most unusual and delightful facts of our world, revelation after revelation.

Begin your journey right now. Open a page at random and dive into a story that will make you wonder, laugh, and even reflect. Your exploration of the world of knowledge is just beginning!

Dino Wonders

- ☐ Tyrannosaurus Rex's Vision: The T-Rex had excellent vision. Its eyes faced forward, giving it depth perception, crucial for a predator.

- ☐ Dinosaur Eggs: Some dinosaur eggs were as big as basketballs. The bigger the egg, the thicker the shell. So, dinosaur eggs were never bigger than about the size of a basketball.

- ☐ Dinosaur Lifespan: Some dinosaurs lived as long as 300 years. However, determining the exact lifespan of dinosaurs is challenging for paleontologists.

- ☐ Feathers on Dinosaurs: Some dinosaurs, like Velociraptors, had feathers. This discovery has changed the way we picture these ancient creatures.

- ☐ The First Dinosaur Fossil: The first-ever recorded dinosaur fossil was found in 1677. It was a thigh bone, but people didn't know it belonged to a dinosaur at that time.

- ☐ Dinosaur Extinction: The most popular theory about dinosaur extinction is the asteroid impact, which created a chain of environmental changes.

- ☐ Colorful Dinosaurs: Recent studies suggest that dinosaurs might have been very colorful, like birds. But we still don't know for sure what colors they were.

- ☐ The Smallest Dinosaur: The smallest known dinosaur was the Microraptor, which was about the size of a pigeon.

- ☐ Dinosaur Brains: Despite their size, many large dinosaurs had brains the size of a walnut, indicating that they weren't very intelligent.

- ☐ Herbivorous Giants: The largest dinosaurs were herbivores (plant eaters), like the Brachiosaurus and Apatosaurus.

- [ ] Dinosaurs and Gravity: Some scientists believe that dinosaurs were so large because the gravity on Earth was weaker in their time.

- [ ] Dinosaur Tail: Dinosaurs used their tails for balance when running and as a defense weapon against predators.

- [ ] Dinosaur Footprints: The longest track of dinosaur footprints ever found is over 1.5 kilometers long and shows the journey of a herd.

- [ ] The Fastest Dinosaur: The fastest dinosaur was the Ornithomimus, which could run up to 70 km/h.

- [ ] Underwater Dinosaurs: There were no underwater dinosaurs. The swimming creatures during the dinosaur era were not dinosaurs, but reptiles like Plesiosaurs and Ichthyosaurs.

- [ ] Dinosaur Growth: Some dinosaurs grew their entire life, getting larger as they aged.

- [ ] Dinosaur Sounds: Scientists believe that dinosaurs could have made sounds but what those sounds were like is still a mystery.

- [ ] Continental Drift: During the dinosaur era, the continents were in different positions, affecting climate and dinosaur migration.

- [ ] Carnivorous Dinosaurs: Carnivorous dinosaurs, like the T-Rex, had serrated teeth, which helped them tear through flesh.

- [ ] Dinosaur Names: Most dinosaur names are in Latin or Greek and describe something about the dinosaur, like its appearance or where it was found.

Wild Wonders

- ☐ Elephant Trunks: An elephant's trunk is incredibly versatile. It can sense the size, shape, and temperature of an object, and is strong enough to lift a tree trunk, yet delicate enough to pick up a blade of grass.

- ☐ Giraffes' Tongues: A giraffe's tongue is about 45-50 cm long and is a dark blue-black color, which is thought to help protect it from sunburn.

- ☐ Cheetahs' Speed: Cheetahs are the fastest land animals, reaching speeds up to 75 mph in just a few seconds, but they can only maintain this incredible speed for short distances.

- ☐ The Blue Whale: The blue whale is the largest animal ever to have lived on Earth, even bigger than the largest dinosaurs. Their heart is as big as a small car!

- ☐ Penguins' Camouflage: Penguins' black and white plumage serves as camouflage while swimming. The black back blends with the dark ocean water when viewed from above, and the white belly matches the brighter ocean surface when seen from below.

- ☐ Octopus Intelligence: Octopuses are highly intelligent; they can solve complex problems, escape from enclosures, and even use tools.

- ☐ The Color-Changing Chameleon: Chameleons change their skin color not just for camouflage but also to express their mood, temperature, and to communicate with other chameleons.

- ☐ Kangaroos' Hopping: Kangaroos can't walk backwards and are the only large animals that hop as a primary means of locomotion. Their strong hind legs and feet are designed for leaping.

- [ ] The Sleepy Koala: Koalas sleep up to 22 hours a day! They need this much rest due to their low-energy diet of eucalyptus leaves.

- [ ] Camels' Humps: A camel's hump does not store water. It stores fat, which they can use as energy when food is scarce.

- [ ] The Arctic Fox: The Arctic fox's fur changes color with the seasons. It turns white in winter for snow camouflage and brown during the summer.

- [ ] Bats' Echolocation: Bats are not blind; they use echolocation to navigate and find food in the dark, emitting sounds and listening for the echoes.

- [ ] Hummingbirds' Flight: Hummingbirds are the only birds that can fly backwards. Their wings move in a figure-eight pattern, allowing them this unique ability.

- [ ] Frog's Life Cycle: Frogs undergo an amazing transformation during their life cycle, from eggs to tadpoles, and then to adult frogs.

- [ ] The Slow Sloth: Sloths are incredibly slow due to their low-energy diet of leaves. They move so little that algae can grow on their fur.

- [ ] Tigers' Unique Stripes: Every tiger has a unique pattern of stripes, much like human fingerprints, which can be used to identify individuals.

- [ ] Dolphins' Communication: Dolphins communicate using a variety of sounds and whistles. They have even been observed to have names, called signature whistles, for each other.

- [ ] The Regenerating Starfish: Starfish can regenerate lost arms, and in some cases, an entire new starfish can grow from a single severed limb.

- [ ] Butterflies' Taste Sensors: Butterflies taste with their feet. They have sensors on their legs that help them find food.

☐ The Immortal Jellyfish: The Turritopsis dohrnii jellyfish can revert back to its juvenile form after reaching adulthood, potentially giving it the ability to live indefinitely.

Pets' Peculiarities

☐ Cats' Whiskers: Cats use their whiskers to measure gaps. The whiskers are roughly as wide as the cat's body, helping them figure out if they can fit through tight spaces.

☐ Dogs' Sense of Smell: A dog's sense of smell is about 40 times better than humans. They can detect odors we can't even begin to notice!

☐ Goldfish Memory: Contrary to popular belief, goldfish have a memory span of several months, not just a few seconds. They can be trained to perform tricks.

☐ Parrots' Lifespan: Some parrot species can live for over 60 years, making them lifelong companions.

☐ Rabbits' Teeth: A rabbit's teeth never stop growing. They keep them worn down by constantly gnawing on hay, vegetables, and other foods.

☐ Hamsters' Cheek Pouches: Hamsters can store food in their cheek pouches, which can stretch to the size of their whole body!

☐ Horses' Communication: Horses communicate with each other through facial expressions, vocal sounds, and body language.

☐ Guinea Pigs' Social Life: Guinea pigs are social creatures that thrive in the company of other guinea pigs and can become lonely and depressed if kept alone.

- ☐ Ferrets' Sleep Habits: Ferrets sleep for about 18 hours a day and are most active during dawn and dusk.

- ☐ Turtles' Longevity: Some pet turtle species can live for several decades, with proper care, making them a long-term commitment as a pet.

- ☐ Birds' Singing Skills: Birds can learn to sing specific tunes. Some can even mimic human speech or household sounds.

- ☐ Lizards' Shedding: Many lizard species shed their skin in large pieces or even whole, unlike snakes, which typically shed their skin in one piece.

- ☐ Cats' Righting Reflex: Cats have a unique ability to twist their bodies mid-air to land on their feet, known as the "righting reflex."

- ☐ Dogs' Dreaming: Dogs experience REM sleep, the stage that humans dream in. They can have dreams and even nightmares.

- ☐ Betta Fish's Individuality: Each Betta fish has its unique personality. Some are aggressive, while others are more peaceful and shy.

- ☐ Rats' Intelligence: Rats are highly intelligent and can be taught tricks and to navigate mazes. They are also very social and affectionate with their human handlers.

- ☐ Pigs' Cleanliness: Contrary to popular belief, pigs are very clean animals. They keep their sleeping areas separate from their bathroom areas.

- ☐ Goats' Pupils: Goats have rectangular pupils, which give them a wide field of vision to watch for predators.

- ☐ Snakes' Eating Habits: Some snakes can eat prey larger than their heads thanks to their flexible jaws.

- ☐ Chickens' Pecking Order: Chickens establish a "pecking order," which is a hierarchy of dominance and social standing within the group.

Deep Dwellers

- ☐ Giant Squid's Eye: The giant squid has the largest eye in the animal kingdom, measuring up to 10 inches in diameter. It's almost the size of a dinner plate!

- ☐ Anglerfish's Lure: The deep-sea anglerfish has a glowing part on its head that it uses to attract prey in the dark ocean depths.

- ☐ Blue Whale's Heart: The heart of a blue whale is so big that a small child could swim through its arteries.

- ☐ Jellyfish's Agelessness: Some jellyfish species are effectively immortal. They can revert back to their juvenile polyp stage after reaching maturity.

- ☐ Vampire Squid's Name: Despite its name, the vampire squid doesn't suck blood. It gets its name from its dark color and webbed arms.

- ☐ Bioluminescence: Many deep-sea creatures, like the firefly squid, create their own light through a chemical reaction, known as bioluminescence, to communicate or attract prey.

- ☐ The Immense Pressure: At the deepest part of the ocean, the pressure is so intense that it's equivalent to having 50 jumbo jets piled on top of you.

- ☐ Blobfish's Appearance: The blobfish looks like a normal fish underwater, but when brought to the surface, it becomes a gooey blob due to the change in pressure.

- ☐ The Colossal Squid: The colossal squid is the largest invertebrate on Earth, with tentacles believed to reach up to 46 feet.

- ☐ Sea Cucumbers' Defense: Some sea cucumbers can expel their internal organs to distract predators and then regrow them.

- ☐ Gulper Eel's Mouth: The gulper eel can swallow prey much larger than itself thanks to its huge, expandable mouth.

- ☐ Dumbo Octopus: Named after the Disney character, the Dumbo octopus uses its ear-like fins to gently move through the water.

- ☐ The Hydrothermal Vents: Deep under the sea, there are hydrothermal vents that shoot out superheated water, creating unique ecosystems filled with specialized creatures.

- ☐ The Pompeii Worm: This worm lives near hydrothermal vents and can withstand some of the hottest temperatures of any marine animal.

- ☐ The Barreleye Fish: This fish has a transparent head, and its eyes can look straight up through it to see prey above.

- ☐ Sea Pig's Eating Habit: The sea pig, a type of sea cucumber, walks along the ocean floor using tentacle-like legs and feeds on decomposing organic matter.

- ☐ The Megamouth Shark: This rare shark has a gigantic mouth and is one of only three known filter-feeding shark species.

- ☐ Christmas Tree Worms: These colorful worms look like tiny Christmas trees and pop out of holes they've bored in coral.

- ☐ The Lanternfish's Light: Lanternfish have light-producing organs to help them attract mates and prey in the deep dark waters.

- ☐ Mantis Shrimp's Punch: The mantis shrimp can punch with the force of a bullet, using its club-like appendages to attack prey.

Insect Insights

- ☐ Butterflies' Taste: Butterflies taste with their feet. They have special sensors on their legs to help them find their favorite plants.

- ☐ Ants' Strength: Ants can lift objects 50 times their body weight. Imagine a human lifting a small car!

- ☐ Fireflies' Glow: Fireflies produce a chemical reaction inside their bodies to glow. This light is used to attract mates and communicate.

- ☐ Dragonflies' Flight: Dragonflies can fly straight up, down, and hover like a helicopter. Their flight is so skilled that they catch 95% of their prey!

☐ Bees' Communication: Bees communicate through a "waggle dance" to tell other bees where to find the best nectar.

☐ Ladybugs' Appetite: A single ladybug can eat up to 5,000 aphids in its lifetime, making them beneficial for gardens.

☐ Caterpillars' Transformation: Caterpillars completely liquefy in the cocoon before turning into a butterfly or moth. It's one of nature's most amazing transformations.

☐ Mosquitoes' Preference: Mosquitoes are more attracted to people with type O blood and those who just exercised, possibly due to the lactic acid in their sweat.

☐ Spiders' Silk: Spider silk is stronger than steel of the same thickness and can stretch up to four times its length.

☐ Crickets' Chirp: Crickets chirp by rubbing their wings together. The number of chirps can tell you the temperature outside.

☐ Fleas' Jump: Fleas can jump up to 150 times their body length, equivalent to a human jumping over 300 meters.

☐ Praying Mantis' Head Rotation: A praying mantis can rotate its head 180 degrees to scan its surroundings.

☐ The Longest Insect: The world's longest insect is the giant stick insect, measuring over 24 inches.

☐ Termites' Mounds: Some termite mounds can reach up to 30 feet tall, the equivalent of a three-story building.

- [ ] Cicadas' Lifespan: Some cicadas live underground for 17 years before emerging for just a few weeks to reproduce.

- [ ] Beetles' Diversity: Beetles are the most diverse group of insects, with over 350,000 known species.

- [ ] Locusts' Swarms: Locusts can form massive swarms that travel long distances, devastating crops.

- [ ] The Death's-Head Hawkmoth: This moth is known for its skull-like pattern on its back and its ability to emit a loud squeak.

- [ ] Butterfly Wings' Colors: Butterflies don't have pigment in their wings. The colors are produced by the light reflecting on their tiny scale structures.

- [ ] Wasps' Paper Nests: Wasps chew wood into a pulp to construct their paper-like nests.

Beastly Feats

- [ ] Peregrine Falcon's Dive: The peregrine falcon is the fastest bird, diving at speeds of over 240 mph (386 km/h) to catch its prey mid-air.

- [ ] The Long-Lived Turtle: Some species of turtles have lifespans that can exceed 150 years, making them one of the longest-living vertebrates.

- [ ] Elephant's Weight: The African elephant is the largest land animal, with some males weighing up to 14,000 lbs (6,350 kg).

- [ ] The Tiny Bumblebee Bat: The bumblebee bat is the smallest mammal by size, measuring about the size of a large bumblebee.

☐ Giraffe's Height: Giraffes are the tallest living terrestrial animals, with an average height of 16 to 18 feet (4.9 to 5.5 meters).

☐ Ostrich's Egg: The ostrich lays the largest eggs of any living land animal, with each egg weighing about 3 pounds (1.4 kg).

☐ Ant's Strength: Relative to its size, the ant is one of the strongest creatures, capable of lifting and carrying objects many times its own weight.

☐ Flea's Jump: Fleas can jump up to 100 times their own height, making them the best jumpers in the animal kingdom, relative to body size.

☐ The Loudest Animal: The sperm whale is the loudest animal on Earth. Their clicks have been measured at 230 decibels, louder than a jet engine.

☐ Arctic Tern's Migration: The Arctic tern has the longest migration of any bird, traveling around 25,000 miles (40,000 km) from the Arctic to the Antarctic and back each year.

☐ Colossal Squid's Size: The colossal squid is the largest invertebrate, with the longest tentacles of any squid species.

☐ Hummingbird's Flap: Hummingbirds have the fastest wing-flapping rate, with their wings beating up to 80 times per second during normal flight.

☐ The Slow Sloth: Sloths are the slowest mammals, moving so leisurely that algae grows on their fur.

☐ The Star-Nosed Mole's Speed Eating: The star-nosed mole is the fastest-eating mammal, able to identify and consume food in less than two-tenths of a second.

- [ ] Kangaroo's Long Jump: Kangaroos are the world's longest jumpers among mammals, capable of leaping distances over 30 feet (9 meters) in a single bound.

- [ ] Anaconda's Weight: The green anaconda is the heaviest snake, with some individuals weighing over 550 pounds (250 kg).

- [ ] The High-Flying Rüppell's Vulture: The Rüppell's vulture is the highest-flying bird, known to fly at altitudes of over 37,000 feet (11,278 meters), nearly as high as some commercial airplanes.

- [ ] Basilisk Lizards' Water Walking: The Basilisk lizard, often called the "Jesus lizard," can run on water for short distances, thanks to its unique foot structure and rapid stride.

- [ ] Snail's Slow Pace: The garden snail is one of the slowest creatures on Earth, moving at a leisurely pace of 0.03 miles per hour. Their slow movement is due to their muscular foot contracting and expanding.

- [ ] Sailfish's Swimming Speed: The sailfish is the fastest fish in the ocean, capable of swimming at a speed of up to 68 miles per hour (110 km/h), making it a swift and efficient predator.

- [ ] The Loudest Insect: The African cicada holds the record for being the loudest insect in the world. Its song can reach an astonishing 106 decibels, which is as loud as a chainsaw.

- [ ] The Tallest Dog Breed: The Great Dane is known for its towering height. The tallest recorded Great Dane, named Zeus, stood at 44 inches (1.12 meters) from paw to shoulder.

Animal Talents

- [ ] Octopuses' Camouflage: Octopuses can change their skin color and texture in seconds to blend into their surroundings, making them masters of disguise.

- [ ] Dolphins' Echolocation: Dolphins use echolocation to navigate and hunt in murky waters. They emit sound waves that bounce off objects, helping them "see" underwater.

- [ ] Geckos' Sticky Feet: Geckos have adhesive toe pads that let them climb smooth surfaces and even walk upside down on ceilings.

- [ ] Bats' Night Vision: Bats aren't blind; they use echolocation to navigate in complete darkness, making high-pitched sounds and listening for the echoes.

- [ ] Cats' Righting Reflex: Cats have an amazing ability to twist their bodies mid-air to land on their feet, known as the "righting reflex."

- [ ] Electric Eels' Shock: Electric eels can generate electric shocks of up to 600 volts to stun prey or defend themselves.

- [ ] Archerfish's Water Shooting: Archerfish can shoot streams of water from their mouths to knock insects off leaves into the water.

- [ ] Birds' Magnetic Vision: Some migratory birds, like pigeons, can sense the Earth's magnetic field, helping them navigate over long distances.

- ☐ Ants' Chemical Communication: Ants communicate and navigate using pheromones, leaving chemical trails for others to follow.

- ☐ Frogs' Freezing Survival: Some frogs can survive being frozen. Their bodies produce a natural antifreeze that prevents ice from damaging their cells.

- ☐ Honeybees' Dance Language: Honeybees perform a "waggle dance" to communicate the direction and distance of food sources to other bees.

- ☐ Chameleons' Tongue: Chameleons have long, sticky tongues that can shoot out at incredible speeds to catch prey.

- ☐ Giraffes' Blood Pressure: Giraffes have a specialized cardiovascular system to manage blood pressure when they lift and lower their heads.

- ☐ Snakes' Infrared Sensing: Pit vipers, pythons, and boas have heat-sensing organs that allow them to detect warm-blooded prey in the dark.

- ☐ Star-Nosed Mole's Touch: The star-nosed mole has 22 tentacle-like appendages on its snout that are incredibly sensitive to touch, helping it find food underground.

- ☐ Cheetahs' Spine Flexibility: Cheetahs have a flexible spine that extends and flexes, allowing for explosive speed and rapid acceleration.

- ☐ Turtles' Long-Distance Navigation: Sea turtles can navigate across thousands of miles of ocean to return to the beaches where they were born.

- ☐ Squirrels' Memory: Squirrels can remember the locations of thousands of nuts they've buried, aiding their survival during winter.

- ☐ Butterflies' Migration: Monarch butterflies migrate thousands of miles, with some traveling from North America to central Mexico.

- ☐ Sloths' Slow Metabolism: Sloths have an extremely slow metabolism, allowing them to survive on a diet of leaves and conserve energy by moving slowly.

Fascinating People

- ☐ Brain Power: The human brain is capable of 1,016 processes per second, making it more powerful than any computer.

- ☐ Unique Fingerprints: Every person has a unique set of fingerprints, and they are formed before birth.

- ☐ Eye Colors: Human eyes can show a vast range of colors, but all blue-eyed people share a common ancestor from about 6,000 to 10,000 years ago.

- ☐ Heartbeats: The average human heart beats around 100,000 times a day, pumping blood to every part of the body.

- ☐ Bone Strength: Human bones are incredibly strong. Ounce for ounce, they're stronger than steel.

- ☐ Taste Buds' Lifespan: Taste buds have a lifespan of about 10 days before new ones replace them.

- ☐ Dreams: Everyone dreams, although we may not remember them. On average, a person can dream for about two hours every night.

- ☐ Blinking: Humans blink approximately 15-20 times per minute. That's over 10 million blinks in a year!

- ☐ Genetic Code: If you could unravel all the DNA in your body, it would stretch to the sun and back over 300 times.

- ☐ Body Heat: The human body generates enough heat in 30 minutes to boil a half-gallon of water.

- ☐ Stomach Acid: Your stomach acid is strong enough to dissolve metal. Thankfully, the stomach renews its lining frequently to prevent digestion of itself.

- ☐ Breath Holding: The world record for holding one's breath underwater is over 24 minutes.

- ☐ Tongue Print: Like fingerprints, each person also has a unique tongue print.

- ☐ Hair Growth: Hair is the second fastest growing tissue in the human body, with bone marrow being the first.

- ☐ Sneezing Speed: A sneeze can travel at speeds of up to 100 miles per hour.

- ☐ Blood Vessels Length: If all the blood vessels in the human body were laid end to end, they would circle the Earth four times.

- ☐ Cell Regeneration: The human body regenerates an entirely new set of skin cells every 27 days.

- ☐ Tears and Emotions: Humans are the only species known to cry as a response to emotional stress or happiness.

☐ Memory Capacity: The human brain's memory capacity is equivalent to more than four terabytes on a hard drive.

☐ Laughing: Laughter is a universal human language. Everyone understands a laugh, regardless of the spoken language.

Human Marvels

☐ Incredible Brain Processing: The human brain can process an image seen for as little as 13 milliseconds, faster than the blink of an eye.

☐ Adaptable Lungs: Human lungs can adapt to high altitudes, increasing their capacity to absorb more oxygen.

☐ Superb Endurance: Humans can outrun many animals over long distances, thanks to our ability to sweat and cool off while running.

☐ Underwater Adaptation: With training, humans can hold their breath underwater for extended periods, a phenomenon enhanced by the 'mammalian dive reflex'.

☐ Hyperelastic Skin: Some people have a condition called Ehlers-Danlos Syndrome, which gives them hyperelastic skin that can stretch much more than usual.

☐ Bone Resilience: Human bones are incredibly resilient and can heal themselves by creating new bone tissue when they break.

☐ Exceptional Fine Motor Skills: The human hand has the ability to perform extremely delicate and complex movements, particularly due to the opposable thumbs.

- [ ] Rapid Healing Skin: Human skin is a fast-healing organ, with the ability to repair minor cuts and abrasions relatively quickly.

- [ ] Flexibility: Some individuals exhibit extraordinary flexibility, allowing them to perform contortions and extraordinary body positions.

- [ ] Night Vision Adaptation: Human eyes can adapt to see in near-total darkness after about 30 minutes, thanks to the rod cells in the retina.

- [ ] High Altitude Survival: Some humans, like those who live in the Himalayas, have adapted to live at high altitudes with lower oxygen levels.

- [ ] Tetrachromacy: Some people, particularly women, have a fourth type of cone cell in their eyes, allowing them to see millions of more colors.

- [ ] Sonic Hearing: Certain individuals have a heightened sense of hearing, enabling them to detect sounds that most people can't hear.

- [ ] Super Tasters: Some people have a heightened sense of taste, making them "super tasters" with a greater sensitivity to flavors.

- [ ] Photographic Memory: A rare ability in humans, photographic memory allows some to remember images, sounds, and objects in great detail.

- [ ] Incredible Reflexes: Some people have exceptionally quick reflexes, enabling them to react to stimuli much faster than the average person.

- [ ] Synesthesia: This unique condition blends senses together, such as seeing sounds as colors or tasting words, providing a unique perception of the world.

- [ ] Extreme Temperature Resistance: Certain individuals can withstand extreme cold or heat due to genetic factors or extensive training.

- [ ] Ultradian Rhythms: Some people can sleep in short bursts throughout the day, a phenomenon known as ultradian rhythms, maximizing their efficiency.

- [ ] Superior Oxygen Usage: Elite athletes can use oxygen more efficiently, allowing them to perform high-intensity activities for longer periods.

Circulatory Secrets

- [ ] Heart Beats: In a lifetime, the average human heart beats more than 2.5 billion times, tirelessly pumping blood throughout the body.

- [ ] Miles of Blood Vessels: If stretched out, an adult's blood vessels could circle Earth's equator four times, covering about 100,000 miles!

- [ ] Blood Cell Journey: A single red blood cell takes only about 20 seconds to circle the whole body.

- [ ] Universal Donor: People with O-negative blood type are universal donors, meaning their blood can be given to people of any blood type.

- [ ] Capillary Size: Capillaries, the smallest blood vessels, are so narrow that red blood cells must travel through them in single file.

- ☐ Pumping Power: Each day, the heart pumps about 2,000 gallons (7,571 liters) of blood.

- ☐ Bone Marrow's Role: Your bone marrow produces about 500 billion blood cells every day.

- ☐ The 'Second Heart': Your calf muscles are often called the 'second heart' due to their role in pumping blood back to the heart from the lower body.

- ☐ Blood Volume: The human body contains about 1.2-1.5 gallons (4.5-5.5 liters) of blood, which is about 7-8% of your body weight.

- ☐ Speedy Blood Cells: Red blood cells can make the entire trip around your body in less than a minute.

- ☐ Lifespan of Blood Cells: Red blood cells live about 120 days, while white blood cells can live from a few days to more than a year.

- ☐ The Sound of Your Heartbeat: The 'lub-dub' sound of your heartbeat is made by your heart valves as they open and close.

- ☐ Blood Pressure Wonders: Blood pressure can be influenced by various factors like stress, diet, exercise, and even the time of day.

- ☐ Platelets and Healing: Platelets in your blood help to stop bleeding when you get a cut by forming clots.

- ☐ Oxygen Transport: Red blood cells transport oxygen from your lungs to tissues throughout your body and return carbon dioxide to be exhaled.

☐ Varied Blood Types: Besides the well-known A, B, AB, and O blood types, there are more than 600 other known antigens that can determine blood type.

☐ Blood's pH Level: The pH level of human blood is tightly regulated and usually stays between 7.35 and 7.45, slightly alkaline.

☐ Veins' One-Way Valves: Veins have one-way valves that keep blood flowing towards the heart, preventing backflow.

☐ The 'Blue Blood' Myth: Human blood is never blue. It appears blue under the skin because of the way light penetrates the skin and is reflected back.

☐ Circulatory and Immune System Link: The circulatory system works closely with the immune system to deliver immune cells to where they are needed.

Senses and Perception

☐ Eyes' Adaptability: Human eyes can adapt to the brightest sunlight and the dimmest moonlight, a range of light nearly a billion times brighter or darker.

☐ Taste Buds Beyond Tongue: Taste buds aren't just on your tongue; they're also on the roof of your mouth and even in your throat.

☐ Super Skin Sensitivity: Your skin is so sensitive that if you were blindfolded, you could feel the wing of a bee on it, just by the pressure it exerts.

☐ Sound Wave Bones: The smallest bones in your body are in your ears (the malleus, incus, and stapes) and they transmit sound waves to your inner ear.

- ☐ The Nose's Memory: The human nose can remember up to 50,000 different scents and it's more sensitive to smells when you're hungry.

- ☐ Eyes' Rapid Movement: Your eyes are constantly moving in quick, tiny movements called microsaccades, helping with stabilizing your vision.

- ☐ Taste and Smell Link: About 80% of what we think is taste is actually smell. That's why food tastes bland when you have a cold.

- ☐ The Decoy Effect in Choices: The human brain is susceptible to a cognitive bias called the "decoy effect," where an additional choice can change our perception of the other options.

- ☐ Color Perception Variance: Not everyone sees colors the same way. For example, what some people see as blue, others may see as green.

- ☐ Touch and Emotions: Gentle touch stimulates the release of oxytocin, a hormone that promotes feelings of trust and bonding.

- ☐ Perceptual Constancy: Our brains maintain a stable perception of objects even as the images on our retinas change; this is why a door appears rectangular even when it's open and the image is trapezoidal.

- ☐ Synesthesia: Some people experience a blending of senses, a phenomenon called synesthesia, where they might see sounds as colors or taste shapes.

- ☐ Peripheral Vision's Sensitivity: Human peripheral vision is more sensitive to light and movement than the detailed vision you use to read or recognize faces.

- [ ] The Illusion of Continuity: The brain automatically fills in gaps in your vision, creating a continuous picture of the world, even though you blink about 15 times a minute.

- [ ] Phantom Limb Sensation: Some people who have lost a limb still feel its presence, known as phantom limb sensation. They can feel pain, itching, or even the sensation of movement.

- [ ] Involuntary Memory Triggers: Smells can trigger more vivid emotional memories than sounds or images, due to the olfactory system's direct connection to the limbic system, the emotional center of the brain.

- [ ] Tickling Yourself: It's almost impossible to tickle yourself because your brain predicts the sensations when your own movement causes them.

- [ ] Hearing Decay with Age: The ability to hear high-pitched sounds declines with age, a condition known as presbycusis.

- [ ] Blind Sight: Some visually impaired people can unconsciously sense objects around them, a phenomenon known as blindsight.

- [ ] Temperature Tactile Illusion: If you touch a piece of metal and a piece of wood in a cold room, the metal feels colder, but in reality, they are the same temperature. This is because metal conducts heat away from your skin more quickly.

Sleep and Its Functions

- [ ] Dream Diversity: Every night, you can have anywhere from 4 to 6 dreams. However, you may not always remember them.

- ☐ Sleep Paralysis: During rapid eye movement (REM) sleep, your muscles are temporarily paralyzed, a natural prevention from acting out your dreams.

- ☐ Sleep for Growth: Growth hormones are primarily released during sleep, which is why good sleep is essential, especially for children and teenagers.

- ☐ Memory Consolidation: Sleep plays a crucial role in memory consolidation, where your brain processes and solidifies what you've learned during the day.

- ☐ Lucid Dreaming: Lucid dreaming is when you're aware that you're dreaming and sometimes can control the narrative of your dream.

- ☐ REM Sleep: REM sleep is the phase when most dreaming occurs. Your eyes move rapidly in various directions during this stage, hence the name.

- ☐ Sleepwalking Mysteries: Sleepwalking usually occurs during deep sleep and can be triggered by lack of sleep, fever, or stress.

- ☐ Napping Benefits: Short naps can boost your mood, alertness, and performance. However, long naps can make it harder to sleep at night.

- ☐ Sleep Deprivation Effects: Lack of sleep can affect your mood, memory, and judgment. Chronic sleep deprivation can lead to serious health issues.

- ☐ The Yawn Cooling Effect: Yawning helps cool down your brain, which is why it's more common before bed and after waking up.

- ☐ Body Temperature Drop: Your body temperature drops slightly when you sleep, which is why a cool room can help you sleep better.

☐ Sleep Position Meaning: Your favorite sleeping position can say a lot about your personality. For example, those who sleep on their back may be more reserved, while side sleepers can be more relaxed and social.

☐ The Purpose of Dreams: Dreams help process emotions and solve problems from your day. They can be a mix of memories, hopes, fears, and random brain signals.

☐ Sleepwalking Conversations: Sleep talkers can have entire conversations while asleep, but they usually won't remember them.

☐ The Half-Asleep Brain: During the first and last five minutes of sleep, you're in a state called hypnagogia, where you're half asleep and half awake.

☐ Circadian Rhythm: Your body follows a natural sleep-wake cycle known as the circadian rhythm, which is influenced by light.

☐ Sleep and Learning: A good night's sleep after learning something new can strengthen neural connections, making the learning process more effective.

☐ The Need for Sleep: While adults need 7-9 hours of sleep per night, teenagers need about 8-10 hours, and younger children need even more.

☐ Dream Color: Not everyone dreams in color. Some people dream only in black and white.

☐ Snoring Facts: Snoring occurs when the flow of air through your mouth and nose is partially blocked during sleep. It's more common in men and overweight individuals.

Human Evolution

- ☐ African Origin: All humans originally evolved in Africa. Our species, Homo sapiens, began to spread across the globe from there about 60,000 years ago.

- ☐ Walking Upright: One of the key steps in human evolution was learning to walk upright. This change freed our hands for using tools.

- ☐ The First Tools: The earliest known human tools were made 2.6 million years ago. They were simple, like sharp-edged stones for cutting meat.

- ☐ Brain Size Increase: Over millions of years, the human brain has tripled in size. The modern human brain is not only larger but also more complex.

- ☐ Fire Control: Humans were the first species to control fire, around 1 million years ago. This helped in cooking food, which made it easier to eat and digest, aiding brain growth.

- ☐ Neanderthals and Us: We once shared the planet with other human-like species, such as Neanderthals. In fact, many of us carry a small percentage of Neanderthal DNA!

- ☐ Loss of Fur: Our ancient ancestors were much hairier. Over time, we lost most of our body hair and developed sweat glands to keep cool while hunting and gathering.

- ☐ Language Development: The ability to speak is a unique human trait. Our vocal cords and the brain's language center have evolved to enable complex speech.

- ☐ Agricultural Revolution: About 10,000 years ago, humans began to farm, leading to the establishment of permanent settlements and a population boom.

- ☐ Domesticating Dogs: Dogs were the first animals to be domesticated by humans, from their wild ancestors, wolves.

- ☐ Lactose Tolerance: Originally, all humans were lactose intolerant. The ability to digest lactose as adults evolved in dairy farming communities about 7,500 years ago.

- ☐ Diverse Skin Colors: Human skin color evolved as a response to varying levels of sunlight in different parts of the world, affecting vitamin D production and UV protection.

- ☐ Sickle Cell Mutation: The sickle cell trait, a mutation in red blood cells, evolved as a protection against malaria, a common disease in Africa.

- ☐ Appendix Evolution: The appendix was once used for digesting tough plant material. Now it's largely redundant, but it can still cause appendicitis.

- ☐ Bipedalism's Downsides: Walking on two legs led to certain disadvantages, like backaches and the pain of childbirth, due to changes in the pelvic structure.

- ☐ Evolution of Laughter: Laughter likely evolved as a way to build social bonds and express relief after stressful situations.

- ☐ Increased Life Expectancy: Modern medicine and improved living conditions have significantly increased human life expectancy, a change that's occurred very rapidly in evolutionary terms.

- [ ] Blue Eyes Are Recent: Blue eyes are a relatively recent development in human history, appearing about 6,000-10,000 years ago due to a genetic mutation.

- [ ] Wisdom Teeth Woes: As human diets changed, our jaws grew smaller. Now, many people don't have enough room for their wisdom teeth, leading to dental issues.

- [ ] Fingerprints for Grip: Fingerprints evolved to improve grip and tactile sensing. Each person's fingerprint pattern is unique and formed before birth.

Cultural Kaleidoscope

- [ ] Japan's Cherry Blossoms: In Japan, the arrival of cherry blossoms, known as 'Sakura', is celebrated with 'Hanami' picnics under the blooming trees, symbolizing the beauty and transience of life.

- [ ] Iceland's Midnight Sun: In Iceland, during summer, the sun sets just before midnight and rises again by 3 am. This phenomenon is celebrated with outdoor activities and festivals.

- [ ] India's Festival of Colors: In India, Holi, the festival of colors, celebrates the arrival of spring. People throw colored powders and water at each other, symbolizing joy and the victory of good over evil.

- [ ] Italy's Leaning Tower: In Pisa, Italy, the Leaning Tower is famous not just for its unintended tilt but also for its role in the development of scientific theories by Galileo.

- [ ] Mongolia's Nomadic Culture: In Mongolia, many people still lead nomadic lifestyles, moving their homes, known as 'gers' or 'yurts', with the seasons.

☐ Australian Aboriginal Culture: Australia's Aboriginal culture is one of the oldest continuous cultures in the world, dating back over 60,000 years with rich traditions, art, and connection to the land.

☐ Brazil's Carnival: Brazil's Carnival is known worldwide for its colorful parades, samba music, and elaborate costumes, reflecting a blend of African, Portuguese, and indigenous cultures.

☐ China's Great Wall: The Great Wall of China, built over centuries to protect against invasions, is the world's longest wall and a symbol of Chinese ingenuity and resilience.

☐ Scottish Kilts: In Scotland, the kilt, a type of knee-length skirt, is a proud symbol of Scottish heritage and is often worn at formal events and celebrations.

☐ Russian Matryoshka Dolls: Matryoshka dolls, or Russian nesting dolls, are a set of wooden dolls of decreasing size placed one inside another, symbolizing motherhood and fertility.

☐ Morocco's Blue City: Chefchaouen, Morocco, is known as the 'Blue City' because many of its buildings are painted in various shades of blue, creating a stunning visual effect.

☐ Mexico's Day of the Dead: Dia de los Muertos (Day of the Dead) in Mexico is a celebration where families welcome back the souls of deceased relatives for a brief reunion with food, drink, and celebration.

☐ Finnish Saunas: In Finland, saunas are a crucial part of culture and social life. Almost every Finnish house has a sauna, used for relaxation and socializing.

- ☐ Greece's Broken Plates: In traditional Greek culture, breaking plates during celebrations is a gesture of joy and friendship, though it's less common now.

- ☐ Egypt's Pyramids: The Pyramids of Egypt are ancient marvels, built as tombs for pharaohs. The Great Pyramid of Giza is one of the Seven Wonders of the Ancient World.

- ☐ French Cuisine: France is renowned for its cuisine, including dishes like escargot, coq au vin, and a variety of cheeses and wines, reflecting a deep appreciation for culinary arts.

- ☐ South African Braai: In South Africa, 'braai' (barbecue) is a popular social event where people gather to cook meat over an open flame and enjoy each other's company.

- ☐ New Zealand's Haka: The Haka, a traditional Māori war dance, is performed at various events in New Zealand, including sports matches, to show strength and unity.

- ☐ Turkish Coffee: In Turkey, coffee is more than a drink; it's a cultural ritual. Turkish coffee is strong, served in small cups, and often accompanied by a sweet treat.

- ☐ Canadian Maple Syrup: In Canada, maple syrup is not just a sweetener but a cultural icon. The country produces about 80% of the world's supply, and its production is celebrated with festivals.

Architectural Marvels

- ☐ Gaudi's Sagrada Familia: In Barcelona, Spain, the Sagrada Familia is a masterpiece by Antoni Gaudi. This unique church, still under construction after over 100 years, combines Gothic and Art Nouveau forms.

- ☐ The Pagodas of Myanmar: Myanmar's landscape is dotted with thousands of pagodas. These tiered towers are typically gilded in gold and are important in Buddhist religious practices.

- ☐ Indonesia's Bamboo Architecture: In Indonesia, architects are using bamboo for its strength and sustainability, creating stunning, eco-friendly structures that blend with nature.

- ☐ Japanese Ryokans: Traditional Japanese inns, called ryokans, are designed for simplicity and tranquility, featuring tatami floors, sliding doors, and communal baths.

- ☐ The White Villages of Andalusia: In southern Spain, the "pueblos blancos" are famous for their whitewashed houses. This style reflects the region's hot climate and Moorish past.

- ☐ Russian Onion Domes: Russia's onion domes, as seen in the Saint Basil's Cathedral in Moscow, are instantly recognizable. They're designed to prevent snow accumulation and symbolize the flame of a candle.

- ☐ Igloos of the Arctic: Inuit people create igloos, dome-shaped structures made of snow blocks. These are surprisingly warm and sturdy, perfect for the Arctic climate.

- ☐ Venice's Floating Palaces: Venice, Italy, is famous for its canals and stately homes called "palazzos" that seem to float on water, reflecting the city's maritime heritage.

- ☐ Moroccan Riads: A riad is a traditional Moroccan house with an interior garden or courtyard. These homes are designed for privacy and relaxation.

- [ ] Feng Shui in Chinese Architecture: Feng Shui, an ancient Chinese philosophy, influences building design in China, focusing on harmony with the surrounding environment.

- [ ] Tibetan Monasteries: Perched high in the Himalayas, Tibetan monasteries are colorful and fortified, reflecting both the Buddhist culture and the need for protection.

- [ ] Indian Stepwells: Stepwells are unique to India. These are wells or ponds in which the water can be reached by descending a set of steps. They are often intricately carved and serve as gathering places.

- [ ] Norwegian Stave Churches: These medieval wooden churches show Viking craftsmanship and are characterized by their timber framing and steep roofs.

- [ ] The Trulli of Alberobello: In Italy, the town of Alberobello is known for its trulli houses, white, cone-roofed buildings that were built without mortar.

- [ ] Greek Island Architecture: The Greek islands are known for their white buildings with blue domes and doors, reflecting the colors of the sea and sky.

- [ ] Victorian Houses in San Francisco: The "Painted Ladies" of San Francisco are Victorian and Edwardian houses painted in bright colors, highlighting their architectural details.

- [ ] Adobe Houses of the American Southwest: These homes are made from a mixture of earth and organic materials, reflecting the native Pueblo Indian styles.

- [ ] Ottoman Mosques in Turkey: The grand mosques of the Ottoman Empire, such as the Blue Mosque in

Istanbul, are known for their large domes, minarets, and elaborate decorations.

- [ ] Mud Houses of Mali: The Great Mosque of Djenné in Mali is the largest mud-brick building in the world, showcasing a distinctive Sudano-Sahelian architectural style.

- [ ] The Bauhaus Movement: Originating in Germany, Bauhaus architecture emphasizes functionality and simplicity, with an absence of ornamentation, influencing modern design worldwide.

Language Mosaic

- [ ] Papua New Guinea's Languages: Papua New Guinea holds the record for the most languages spoken in a single country, with over 800 distinct languages!

- [ ] India's Linguistic Diversity: India is a linguistic treasure trove with 22 officially recognized languages and hundreds more spoken across the country.

- [ ] Vanishing Languages: Every two weeks, a language dies with its last fluent speaker. This loss equals the disappearance of a unique cultural perspective.

- [ ] China's Dialects: Mandarin is just one of many Chinese dialects. Others, like Cantonese and Shanghainese, are so different they're almost like separate languages.

- [ ] The Rosetta Stone: The Rosetta Stone, discovered in Egypt, was key to deciphering Egyptian hieroglyphs because it had the same text in three different scripts, including Ancient Greek.

☐ Language Families: There are about 7,000 languages worldwide, grouped into roughly 150 language families.

☐ Europe's Linguistic Diversity: Europe is incredibly linguistically diverse for its size, with over 200 European languages and many more dialects.

☐ South Africa's Official Languages: South Africa recognizes 11 official languages, one of the highest numbers of official languages in any country.

☐ The Bible's Translations: The Bible is the most translated book in the world, available in hundreds of languages and dialects.

☐ Greenland's Inuit Language: In Greenland, the primary language is Kalaallisut, an Inuit language, which has words that can tell whole stories in a single term.

☐ Ancient Latin's Influence: Latin, though a dead language, is the ancestor of the Romance languages, including Spanish, French, Italian, Portuguese, and Romanian.

☐ Australia's Indigenous Languages: Before European settlement, there were over 250 Indigenous Australian languages. Sadly, many have been lost, but efforts are being made to revive some.

☐ Sign Languages: Sign languages, used by deaf communities, are fully-fledged languages with their own grammar and vocabulary, not just a translation of spoken language.

☐ Switzerland's Multilingualism: Switzerland has four official languages: German, French, Italian, and Romansh, reflecting its cultural diversity.

- ☐ The Sámi Languages: In Northern Europe, the indigenous Sámi people speak languages that are part of the Uralic family, unrelated to Scandinavian languages.

- ☐ Iceland's Language Conservation: Iceland has preserved its language so well that today's Icelanders can still read old Norse texts from centuries ago.

- ☐ Constructed Languages: Some languages are created for fictional worlds, like Klingon in "Star Trek" and Elvish in "The Lord of the Rings."

- ☐ The Complexity of Chinese Characters: A single Chinese character can represent a whole word or concept. There are thousands of characters, making it one of the most complex writing systems.

- ☐ Russian's Cyrillic Alphabet: The Cyrillic alphabet, used in Russian and other Slavic languages, was developed in the 9th century by Saint Cyril and Saint Methodius.

- ☐ The Basque Language Mystery: The Basque language, spoken in a region spanning northeastern Spain and southwestern France, is unique. It's unrelated to any other language and predates the Indo-European languages of Europe.

Facts About Old Games

- ☐ Chess Origins: Chess originated in India around the 6th century AD. Originally called 'Chaturanga', it was a game of strategic skill and represented a battle between two armies.

- ☐ The Royal Game of Ur: One of the oldest known board games is the Royal Game of Ur from ancient

Mesopotamia, dating back to 2600 BC. It's a race game, much like modern backgammon.

- ☐ Mancala's Ancient Roots: Mancala is believed to be one of the oldest games still played today. It was played in Ancient Egypt and involves moving stones around a board of pits.

- ☐ Go's Long History: Originating in China over 2,500 years ago, Go is one of the oldest board games in the world. It's known for its deep strategy despite simple rules.

- ☐ The Viking's Chess - Hnefatafl: Hnefatafl was a popular game among Vikings. It's a strategic, asymmetrical board game where a king tries to escape from a group of attackers.

- ☐ Olympic Games Beginnings: The ancient Olympic Games began in 776 BC in Greece and included events like running, long jump, shot put, javelin, boxing, and equestrian events.

- ☐ Senet - An Egyptian Game: Senet, one of the oldest known board games, was played in Ancient Egypt over 5,000 years ago. It's thought to be a precursor to modern backgammon.

- ☐ Knucklebones - Ancient Dice: Before modern dice, people in many ancient cultures played games with knucklebones from sheep or goats. These were similar to dice and used for games of chance.

- ☐ Roman Ludus Latrunculorum: This ancient Roman game, also known as the Game of Mercenaries, was a military strategy game similar to chess but with different rules and gameplay.

☐ Ancient Greek Petteia: Played by Ancient Greeks, Petteia was a strategic board game considered a precursor to checkers or draughts.

☐ Chinese Xiangqi: Xiangqi, or Chinese chess, dates back to the 10th century and has pieces representing different military units, each with unique movements.

☐ Patolli - Aztec Game of Luck: The Aztecs played a game called Patolli, which was a race game of luck and strategy, played with beans or stones on a cross-shaped board.

☐ Shogi - Japanese Chess: Shogi, the Japanese version of chess, involves a unique feature where captured pieces can be returned to the board under the capturer's control.

☐ The Game of Polo: Originating in Persia around the 6th century BC, Polo was initially a training game for cavalry units. It's one of the world's oldest known team sports.

☐ Ancient Mesoamerican Ballgame: Played over 3,000 years ago, this ballgame was popular among ancient Mesoamerican cultures and was often linked to religious rituals.

☐ Tafl Games: These were a family of ancient Germanic and Celtic board games played across medieval Europe. They were strategic, like chess, but used asymmetrical starting positions.

☐ Nine Men's Morris: This is an ancient alignment game traced back to the Roman Empire. Players aim to form 'mills' or lines of three to remove opponent pieces.

- ☐ Chaturaji - Four-Player Chess: An ancient Indian variant of chess, Chaturaji was played by four people and involved an element of chance, introduced by rolling dice.

- ☐ Ancient Egyptian Dice: Dice in ancient Egypt were often made from animal bones and had shapes and numbering different from today's cubic dice.

- ☐ Kubb - Viking Chess: Kubb, also known as Viking Chess, is believed to have been played by Vikings. It involves throwing wooden sticks to knock over wooden blocks.

Board Games

- ☐ Monopoly's Hidden History: Monopoly was originally created to demonstrate the evils of land monopolies. It was called 'The Landlord's Game' and had two sets of rules: anti-monopolist and monopolist.

- ☐ The Longest Monopoly Game: The longest game of Monopoly ever played lasted 70 straight days!

- ☐ Scrabble's Word Power: There are over 105,000 words in the official Scrabble dictionary. The game was originally named 'Lexiko' and then 'Criss-Crosswords'.

- ☐ Clue/Cluedo's Original Name: The game known as Clue in North America was originally named Cluedo in the UK and was created during World War II.

- ☐ Risk's Creation: Risk, the game of global domination, was invented by a French filmmaker, Albert Lamorisse, in 1957.

- ☐ Catan's Resource Management: Settlers of Catan, a game about trading resources and building settlements, has sold over 22 million copies in 30 languages.

- ☐ Chess's Deep Origins: Chess, one of the oldest games still played, has roots going back about 1,500 years. Its earliest form was in India, known as Chaturanga.

- ☐ The Game of Life's Morals: The Game of Life was originally created in 1860 and was meant to teach moral lessons. The modern version was updated in 1960 to focus more on material success.

- ☐ Pandemic's Teamwork Focus: Unlike most board games, Pandemic is a cooperative game where players work together to stop global outbreaks of diseases.

- ☐ Ticket to Ride's Train Adventure: Ticket to Ride, a railway-themed board game, has won numerous awards and is especially known for its simple rules and strategic depth.

- ☐ Battleship's Early Forms: Battleship was originally a pencil and paper game dating back to World War I. It was later produced as a board game in the 1960s.

- ☐ Twister's Controversy: When Twister was released in 1966, it was initially criticized for being "too suggestive" but later became a hit after being played on 'The Tonight Show'.

- ☐ Jenga's Meaning: The word 'Jenga' is derived from 'kujenga', a Swahili word that means 'to build'. The game was created by Leslie Scott based on wooden blocks from her childhood in Africa.

- ☐ Carcassonne's Medieval Inspiration: The game Carcassonne is named after a medieval fortress in southern France and involves building a landscape with tiles.

☐ The Ouija Board's Patent: The Ouija board was patented in 1891 as a "talking board" and was originally used as a means of supposed communication with the dead.

☐ Operation's Accidental Invention: The game Operation was invented by a university student as a class project. It was initially called 'Death Valley'.

☐ Trivial Pursuit's Creation: Trivial Pursuit was created in 1979 by two Canadian journalists who wanted a game that combined their love of trivia.

☐ Mousetrap's Rube Goldberg Machine: The game Mousetrap, where players build a complex machine to catch mice, is based on the whimsical inventions of cartoonist Rube Goldberg.

☐ Candy Land's Sweet Origins: Candy Land was created in 1948 by a schoolteacher as a game for children recovering from polio, which explains its simplicity.

☐ Dungeons & Dragons' Fantasy World: Dungeons & Dragons, the first role-playing game, was published in 1974, blending medieval fantasy with complex storytelling and character-building.

World Records in Gaming

☐ World's Largest Chess Piece: The world's largest chess piece is a king, standing at over 20 feet tall in St. Louis, Missouri, the chess capital of the U.S.

☐ Most Expensive Video Game Ever Developed: "Grand Theft Auto V" holds the record for the most expensive video game ever developed, with a cost of $265 million.

☐ World's Largest Jigsaw Puzzle: The largest jigsaw puzzle had 551,232 pieces and covered over 29,000 square feet, which is about half the size of a football field.

☐ Longest Gaming Marathon: A Belgian gamer holds the record for the longest gaming marathon, playing for nearly 121 hours straight on a single game.

☐ Fastest Time to Solve a Rubik's Cube: The world record for solving a Rubik's Cube is under 4 seconds. That's faster than it takes to tie your shoelaces!

☐ Largest Collection of Video Games: The largest collection of video games includes over 20,000 unique games. That's more games than you could play in a lifetime!

☐ Highest Earning eSports Player: The highest-earning eSports player has won over $4 million from competitive gaming, showing that playing games can indeed be a lucrative career.

☐ Oldest Board Game Still Played: The game of Go, originating in China over 2,500 years ago, is the oldest board game still played today in its original form.

☐ World's Largest Dungeon & Dragons Game: The largest Dungeons & Dragons game had over 500 players, turning a fantasy adventure into an epic real-world gathering.

☐ Most Played Mobile Game: "Candy Crush Saga" is the most-played mobile game, with millions of people swiping candies daily across the globe.

☐ Fastest Selling Entertainment Product: When released, "Call of Duty: Black Ops II" grossed $500 million in 24 hours, making it the fastest-selling entertainment product at the time.

☐ Longest Pokemon Marathon: A group of gamers played Pokémon for over 300 hours to set a world record for the longest Pokémon marathon.

☐ Highest Score in Pac-Man: The highest possible score in Pac-Man is 3,333,360 points, achieved by eating every dot, fruit, and enemy in each of the 256 levels without losing a life.

☐ World's Largest LAN Party: The world's largest LAN (Local Area Network) party had over 22,000 connected computers, creating a gamer's paradise.

☐ Most Successful Trading Card Game: "Magic: The Gathering" holds the record for the most successful trading card game, with billions of cards printed since its inception in 1993.

☐ Longest Tabletop Game: A game of "Descent: Journeys in the Dark" lasted over 91 hours, a true test of endurance and strategy for the players.

☐ Most Simultaneous Chess Games: A grandmaster set a record by playing simultaneous chess games, winning 88% of them.

☐ Largest "Minecraft" Pixel Art: The largest Minecraft pixel art consists of over 1.1 million blocks, showcasing incredible dedication and creativity.

☐ Fastest Time to Beat "Super Mario Bros": The world record for beating the original "Super Mario Bros" is just under 5 minutes, a feat requiring near-perfect play.

- ☐ **Most Played Board Game:** Chess is arguably the most played board game in history, with millions enjoying the game around the globe daily.

- ☐ World's Smallest Rubik's Cube: The smallest working Rubik's Cube measures just 5.6 mm on each side, about the size of a pea.

- ☐ Longest Time Spent in Virtual Reality: A record was set for spending over 36 hours in a virtual reality game, a true immersion into a digital world.

- ☐ Most Participants in a Board Game: An outdoor Dutch version of Monopoly had 733 participants, turning a classic board game into a massive community event.

- ☐ Highest Score in "Tetris": The world record for the highest score in "Tetris" is held by a player who reached over 999,999 points, the game's maximum score.

- ☐ Fastest Completion of "The Legend of Zelda": A gamer completed "The Legend of Zelda: Ocarina of Time" in less than 17 minutes, using intricate knowledge and shortcuts.

- ☐ Most Claps in a Minute: The record for the most claps in one minute is 1,080. That's almost 18 claps per second!

- ☐ Longest "Mario Kart" Marathon: Players set a record by playing "Mario Kart" for over 35 hours straight, a testament to endurance and love for the game.

- ☐ World's Largest "Uno" Game: The largest game of "Uno" involved 2,146 participants, turning this popular card game into a grand social event.

- ☐ Longest Table Tennis Serve: The longest table tennis serve was over 93 feet, almost the length of a basketball court.

- ☐ Largest Collection of Board Games: A German collector holds the record with over 20,000 different board games in his collection.

- ☐ Fastest Time to Stack a Cup Pyramid: The record for stacking a pyramid of cups is just under 5 seconds, showcasing incredible speed and precision.

- ☐ Highest Altitude Scrabble Game: A game of Scrabble was played at the base camp of Mount Everest, over 17,000 feet above sea level.

- ☐ Most Expensive Chess Set: The most expensive chess set is valued at over $9.8 million, made with gold, diamonds, sapphires, and emeralds.

- ☐ Fastest "Minesweeper" Completion: The record for completing the expert level of "Minesweeper" is just over 31 seconds, requiring quick thinking and precision.

- ☐ Most Dominoes Toppled: The most dominoes toppled in one go is over 4 million, creating an incredible spectacle as they fell in sequence.

- ☐ Largest "Risk" Board: The largest "Risk" game board was over 2,500 square feet, turning the game of global domination into a life-sized experience.

- ☐ World's Oldest Gaming Dice: The oldest known gaming dice were found in Iran and are over 5,000 years old, made from carved bone.

- [ ] Longest Continuous Poker Game: A poker game in Arizona lasted over 8 years, with a rotating roster of players, setting a record for endurance.

- [ ] Most Prolific Game Inventor: Ernő Rubik, the inventor of the Rubik's Cube, also created several other puzzles and games, making him one of the most prolific game inventors.

Facts About Esports

- [ ] First eSports Event: The first known eSports event happened in 1972 at Stanford University for the game "Spacewar!" where the winner received a year's subscription to "Rolling Stone" magazine.

- [ ] Largest eSports Prize Pool: The 2019 "Dota 2" International Tournament had the largest prize pool in eSports history, exceeding $34 million.

- [ ] Youngest eSports Champion: A 13-year-old won $1 million in the "Fortnite" World Cup, making him one of the youngest eSports champions ever.

- [ ] eSports in the Asian Games: eSports was a demonstration sport at the 2018 Asian Games and is set to be a medal event in future games, signifying its rising global recognition.

- [ ] eSports Viewership: The 2019 "League of Legends" World Championship Finals had more viewers than the Super Bowl, showcasing the immense popularity of eSports.

- [ ] First Dedicated eSports Arena: The first dedicated eSports arena was opened in Santa Ana, California, in 2015, providing a professional venue for gaming tournaments.

- ☐ Training Regimen of Professional Gamers: Professional gamers often train for 10-12 hours a day, similar to traditional athletes, to hone their skills and reflexes.

- ☐ eSports Scholarships: Universities around the world are now offering scholarships for eSports, recognizing it as a competitive discipline.

- ☐ Global eSports Revenue: eSports is a rapidly growing industry, with global revenues reaching billions of dollars annually, partly from sponsorships and media rights.

- ☐ Widespread Gaming Platforms: eSports competitions are held on various gaming platforms, including PC, consoles, and even mobile games.

- ☐ Diverse Game Genres: eSports covers a wide range of game genres, from multiplayer online battle arenas (MOBAs) to first-person shooters (FPS) and real-time strategy (RTS) games.

- ☐ eSports Coaches: Just like traditional sports, eSports teams often have coaches and analysts who help players improve their strategies and skills.

- ☐ Physical and Mental Fitness: Top eSports players maintain physical and mental fitness routines to enhance concentration, reduce stress, and improve reaction times.

- ☐ Virtual Reality eSports: Emerging VR technology is introducing a new dimension to eSports, with dedicated VR gaming competitions beginning to take place.

- ☐ Female eSports Champions: While eSports has predominantly male participants, female champions are emerging and making a mark in various tournaments.

- ☐ eSports in Television: Major networks like ESPN and BBC have started broadcasting eSports events, further legitimizing it as a competitive sport.

- ☐ eSports Popularity in South Korea: South Korea is often considered the birthplace of professional eSports, with a massive fan base and dedicated TV channels for gaming.

- ☐ eSports Team Houses: Some professional eSports teams live and train together in dedicated team houses, where they can practice strategies and build team chemistry.

- ☐ eSports Mascots and Brands: Just like traditional sports teams, some eSports teams have mascots, merchandise, and a large, dedicated fan base.

- ☐ The Olympic Debate: There is ongoing debate about including eSports in the Olympics, with arguments focusing on whether it should be recognized as a sport like traditional athletic events.

Space Odyssey

- ☐ First Human in Space: Yuri Gagarin, a Soviet astronaut, was the first human to journey into outer space in 1961, orbiting the Earth in Vostok 1.

- ☐ Longest Time in Space: Russian cosmonaut Valeri Polyakov spent the longest continuous time in space – 437 days aboard the Mir space station.

- ☐ Walking on the Moon: Neil Armstrong was the first person to walk on the moon in 1969, famously saying,

"That's one small step for man, one giant leap for mankind."

- [ ] Spacecraft Speed: The fastest-ever spacecraft, the Parker Solar Probe, will reach speeds of 430,000 mph as it approaches the sun.

- [ ] Animals in Space: Before humans went into space, animals like dogs, monkeys, and even fruit flies were sent to test the effects of space travel.

- [ ] Living in Space: Astronauts living on the International Space Station (ISS) experience 16 sunrises and sunsets each day as they orbit the Earth.

- [ ] Space Suit Costs: A single NASA space suit costs $12 million and is made to withstand extreme temperatures and micrometeoroids.

- [ ] Women in Space: In 1963, Valentina Tereshkova became the first woman to fly in space, orbiting the Earth 48 times.

- [ ] Space Food: Early space food was like toothpaste tubes and cubes, but now astronauts eat a variety of foods, including pizza and ice cream.

- [ ] Zero Gravity Effects: In zero gravity, astronauts can grow up to 3% taller during space missions due to spinal lengthening.

- [ ] The Hubble Space Telescope: Launched in 1990, the Hubble Space Telescope has taken some of the most detailed images of distant galaxies, contributing greatly to astronomy.

- ☐ SpaceX's Reusable Rockets: SpaceX developed the Falcon 9, the first reusable rocket, making space travel more sustainable and cost-effective.

- ☐ Satellites Around Earth: There are over 2,000 active satellites orbiting Earth right now, used for communication, weather monitoring, and navigation.

- ☐ The Voyager Probes: Voyager 1 and 2, launched in 1977, are the furthest human-made objects from Earth and have left our solar system.

- ☐ Mars Rovers: Robotic rovers like Curiosity and Perseverance are exploring Mars' surface, sending back valuable data about the planet's geology and climate.

- ☐ Space Junk: There are millions of pieces of space debris, or "space junk", orbiting Earth, including old satellites and fragments from disintegrated spacecraft.

- ☐ The International Space Station: The ISS is a habitable artificial satellite and has been continuously occupied since November 2000, making it a unique laboratory for scientific research.

- ☐ Astronaut Training: Astronauts undergo rigorous training, including underwater spacewalk simulations, to prepare for the challenges of working in space.

- ☐ Sounds in Space: Space is a vacuum, meaning sound can't travel through it. Astronauts use radios to communicate.

- ☐ The First Space Tourist: In 2001, American businessman Dennis Tito became the first space tourist, paying $20 million for a trip to the ISS.

Facts About Planets

- ☐ **Jupiter's Giant Storm:** Jupiter's Great Red Spot is a giant storm larger than Earth that has been raging for at least 400 years.

- ☐ **Venus' Rotation:** Venus has the longest rotation period of any planet in the Solar System and rotates in the opposite direction to most planets.

- ☐ **Saturn's Rings:** Saturn's beautiful rings are made mostly of ice particles, along with some rock debris and dust. They are about 282,000 kilometers wide but only about 1 kilometer thick.

- ☐ **Mars' Volcanoes:** Mars is home to Olympus Mons, the tallest volcano in the Solar System, standing at 22 kilometers high, nearly three times the height of Mount Everest.

- ☐ **Mercury's Craters:** Mercury's surface resembles our Moon, covered with craters from impacts due to its thin atmosphere.

- ☐ **Earth's Moving Continents:** Earth's surface is constantly moving. The continents have been in almost constant motion for millions of years and will continue to shift.

- ☐ **Neptune's Winds:** Winds on Neptune are the fastest in the Solar System, reaching speeds of 2,100 kilometers per hour.

- ☐ **Uranus' Tilt:** Uranus is tilted so far on its side that it orbits the Sun on its side, leading to extreme seasons.

- ☐ Pluto's Heart: Pluto, once considered the ninth planet, has a large heart-shaped glacier the size of Texas and Oklahoma combined.

- ☐ Jupiter's Moons: Jupiter has 79 known moons, the most of any planet in the Solar System. The largest four, known as the Galilean moons, were discovered by Galileo Galilei in 1610.

- ☐ Earth's Liquid Water: Earth is the only known planet in the Solar System with liquid water on its surface.

- ☐ Saturn's Density: Saturn is so light for its size that if you could find an ocean big enough, it would float.

- ☐ Venus' Extreme Heat: Venus is the hottest planet in the Solar System, with surface temperatures hot enough to melt lead.

- ☐ Mars' Iron Oxide: The red color of Mars is due to iron oxide (rust) in its soil.

- ☐ Mercury's Extreme Temperatures: Mercury has the most significant temperature fluctuations of the planets, with temperatures ranging from extremely hot to freezing.

- ☐ Jupiter's Magnetic Field: Jupiter has the strongest magnetic field of any planet in the Solar System, 20 times stronger than Earth's.

- ☐ Neptune's Blue Color: Neptune's vivid blue color is caused by methane in its atmosphere, absorbing red light and reflecting blue light.

- ☐ Uranus' Discovery: Uranus was the first planet discovered with a telescope in 1781 by William Herschel.

☐ Saturn's Moon Titan: Titan, one of Saturn's moons, has thick atmosphere and liquid lakes of methane and ethane, the only other known body in the Solar System with stable liquid on its surface.

☐ Earth's Twin Venus: Venus is often called Earth's twin because of their similar size, mass, proximity to the Sun, and bulk composition. However, its runaway greenhouse effect makes it vastly different from Earth

Cosmic Mysteries

☐ Black Hole's Gravitational Pull: Black holes have such strong gravitational pulls that not even light can escape them, which is why we can't see them directly.

☐ The First Photo of a Black Hole: In 2019, humanity captured the first ever image of a black hole's event horizon, located in the galaxy M87, using a global network of telescopes.

☐ Singularity: At the center of a black hole is the singularity, where matter is thought to be infinitely dense and the laws of physics as we know them cease to operate.

☐ Hawking Radiation: Stephen Hawking theorized that black holes emit radiation due to quantum effects near the event horizon. This radiation is now known as Hawking radiation.

☐ Size of Black Holes: Black holes can vary in size. The smallest, known as 'primordial black holes,' could be as small as a single atom but with the mass of a large mountain.

☐ Supermassive Black Holes: Most galaxies, including our own Milky Way, have a supermassive black hole at their center, which can have a mass equivalent to millions or even billions of suns.

☐ Galactic Cannibals: When galaxies collide, their central black holes can merge to form an even larger black hole, essentially 'cannibalizing' each other.

☐ Black Hole Formation: Black holes are formed from the remnants of massive stars that collapse under their own gravity at the end of their life cycles.

☐ Time Distortion Near Black Holes: Near a black hole, the strong gravitational pull can significantly distort time, in accordance with Einstein's theory of relativity.

☐ Wormholes Theories: Some scientists speculate that black holes could be connected to wormholes – theoretical passages through space-time allowing for travel over vast distances.

☐ Black Hole Jets: Some black holes emit powerful jets of particles, traveling at nearly the speed of light, often perpendicular to their accretion disks.

☐ Spaghettification: If you were to fall into a black hole, the immense gravitational gradient would stretch you out like spaghetti in a process humorously termed "spaghettification."

☐ Quasars: Quasars are extremely bright and distant objects powered by black holes consuming material at the centers of young galaxies.

☐ The Event Horizon: The event horizon of a black hole is the point of no return. Once crossed, nothing, not even light, can escape back into space.

- ☐ Black Holes and Galaxy Evolution: Black holes play a crucial role in the formation and evolution of galaxies, influencing their growth and structure.

- ☐ Black Hole Collisions and Gravitational Waves: When two black holes collide, they can produce ripples in space-time known as gravitational waves, which were first detected in 2015.

- ☐ Dark Matter Mystery: While not directly observable, dark matter is thought to make up about 27% of the universe. Its presence is inferred from its gravitational effects on visible matter and light.

- ☐ The Cosmic Web: The universe contains a vast network of interconnected filaments of dark matter, known as the cosmic web, which structures the universe on its largest scales.

- ☐ Neutron Stars and Black Holes: Neutron stars are the densest stars known, and when they collapse, they can turn into black holes.

- ☐ The Ultimate Fate of Black Holes: According to Hawking's theory, black holes could eventually evaporate over astronomical timescales through Hawking radiation.

Space Weather

- ☐ Solar Flares: Solar flares are sudden explosions on the Sun, releasing huge amounts of energy equivalent to millions of 100-megaton hydrogen bombs exploding at once.

- ☐ Auroras: The Northern and Southern Lights, known as auroras, are caused by solar winds interacting with Earth's magnetic field, creating stunning light displays in the sky.

- ☐ Comets' Tails: Comets have two tails – a dust tail and an ion tail. The ion tail is formed by solar wind pushing ionized gas away from the comet, and it always points away from the Sun.

- ☐ Meteor Showers: When Earth passes through the trail of debris left by a comet, we experience meteor showers as these particles burn up in our atmosphere.

- ☐ The Heliosphere: The heliosphere is a vast bubble around the Sun and planets, formed by the solar wind. It extends far beyond Pluto and acts as a shield against cosmic radiation.

- ☐ Space Lightning: Lightning in space, also known as "sprites" or "elves," can occur on planets like Jupiter and Saturn, and even on the Sun.

- ☐ Blackout Risks from Solar Storms: Large solar flares can cause geomagnetic storms that disrupt satellite communications and power grids on Earth, causing widespread blackouts.

- ☐ Galactic Cosmic Rays: Cosmic rays are high-energy particles originating outside our solar system and can be hazardous to astronauts in deep space.

- ☐ Solar Wind Speed: Solar wind, a stream of charged particles from the Sun, travels at speeds of about 400 kilometers per second (nearly 1 million miles per hour).

- ☐ The Zodiacal Light: The zodiacal light is a faint, diffuse glow in the night sky, caused by sunlight reflecting off dust particles in space between the planets.

☐ Blue Suns and Red Moons: The Sun can appear blue when seen from the edge of our atmosphere, while the Moon can turn red during a lunar eclipse.

☐ The Van Allen Radiation Belts: Earth is surrounded by two layers of charged particles, known as the Van Allen radiation belts, trapped by the planet's magnetic field.

☐ Magnetic Reconnection: This process in space, where magnetic field lines from different magnetic domains are forced together, releases a large amount of energy and can drive solar flares and coronal mass ejections.

☐ Space Weather Forecasting: Just like Earth's weather, space weather can be forecasted to predict solar flares, geomagnetic storms, and other space phenomena.

☐ Coronal Mass Ejections (CMEs): These are large expulsions of plasma and magnetic field from the Sun's corona. They can eject billions of tons of coronal material and carry an embedded magnetic field stronger than Earth's.

☐ Sunspots and Solar Cycles: Sunspots are cooler areas on the Sun's surface with strong magnetic fields. The number of sunspots increases and decreases over an 11-year cycle.

☐ Aurora on Other Planets: Auroras are not exclusive to Earth; they have been observed on other planets in our solar system, including Jupiter and Saturn.

☐ Leonids Meteor Shower: The Leonids meteor shower occurs annually and is known for producing some of the most intense meteor storms in history.

- [ ] Solar Minimum and Maximum: The solar cycle includes a solar minimum, with few sunspots and low solar activity, and a solar maximum, with many sunspots and increased solar activity.

- [ ] Polar Night and Midnight Sun: Near the poles, there is a phenomenon known as polar night and midnight sun, where the sun doesn't rise or set for months, affecting the local space weather.

Galaxies

- [ ] Milky Way's Size: Our galaxy, the Milky Way, is about 100,000 light-years across, meaning that light takes 100,000 years to travel from one end to the other.

- [ ] Galaxies' Variety: There are estimated to be over two trillion galaxies in the observable universe, each with millions to trillions of stars.

- [ ] Andromeda's Collision Course: The Andromeda Galaxy, our closest galactic neighbor, is on a collision course with the Milky Way, expected to merge in about 4 billion years.

- [ ] Spiral Galaxy Arms: Spiral galaxies like the Milky Way have arms winding around their centers. These arms are formed by density waves that compress gas and dust, leading to star formation.

- [ ] The Black Hole at the Center: Most galaxies, including the Milky Way, have supermassive black holes at their centers. Our galaxy's black hole is called Sagittarius A*.

- [ ] Galactic Cannibalism: Larger galaxies grow by absorbing smaller ones, a process known as galactic cannibalism. The Milky Way has consumed several smaller galaxies over its lifetime.

☐ The Oldest Galaxies: The oldest known galaxies formed over 13 billion years ago, just a few hundred million years after the Big Bang.

☐ Barred Spiral Galaxies: About two-thirds of spiral galaxies, including the Milky Way, have a bar-like structure of stars extending from their centers.

☐ Galaxies' Rotating Speeds: Despite their massive size, galaxies can rotate at speeds of up to 225 kilometers per second.

☐ Irregular Galaxies: Not all galaxies have defined shapes. Irregular galaxies lack a distinct form, often resulting from galactic collisions and mergers.

☐ Star Formation in Galaxies: New stars are constantly being born in galaxies. In the Milky Way, about one to three new stars are born each year.

☐ The Color of Galaxies: Young galaxies appear blue due to the light of hot, young stars. Older galaxies appear redder because of their older, cooler stars.

☐ Dwarf Galaxies: Dwarf galaxies are the most common type in the universe. They have fewer stars and are much smaller than galaxies like the Milky Way.

☐ The Hubble Ultra-Deep Field: The Hubble Space Telescope captured an image called the Ultra-Deep Field, showing about 10,000 galaxies in a patch of sky just one-tenth the diameter of the moon.

☐ Galactic Magnetic Fields: Galaxies have their own magnetic fields, generated by the motion of stars, gas, and the galactic core.

☐ Intergalactic Stars: Some stars are found not in galaxies, but in the spaces between them. These are known as intergalactic stars.

☐ Galactic Collisions: When galaxies collide, it's a slow process taking millions of years, and because of vast distances between stars, they rarely collide with each other.

☐ Elliptical Galaxies: These galaxies are shaped like elongated spheres. They have very little dust and gas and are often made up of older stars.

☐ The Sombrero Galaxy: This galaxy is known for its bright core and large central bulge, surrounded by a thin disk of stars and dust, resembling a sombrero hat.

☐ Galactic Evolution: Galaxies evolve over billions of years, changing in shape and size, influenced by gravity, collisions, and the formation of new stars.

UFO Mysteries

☐ The First Recorded UFO Sighting: The first recorded UFO sighting dates back to 1440 BC in ancient Egypt, where scribes recorded seeing fiery disks in the sky.

☐ Roswell Incident: The most famous UFO incident occurred in 1947 in Roswell, New Mexico, where a mysterious object crashed, leading to widespread speculation about alien spacecraft.

☐ Project Blue Book: The U.S. Air Force conducted a study called Project Blue Book from 1952 to 1969, investigating over 12,000 reported UFO sightings.

☐ The Phoenix Lights: In 1997, thousands of people in Phoenix, Arizona, observed a series of strange lights and a large V-shaped craft in the sky, sparking major UFO claims.

☐ UFOs and Presidents: Former U.S. President Jimmy Carter reported seeing a UFO in 1969 and promised more government transparency on UFO information during his presidency.

☐ The UFO Capital of the World: Roswell, New Mexico, claims to be the UFO capital of the world and hosts an annual festival attracting thousands of UFO enthusiasts.

☐ The Belgian UFO Wave: In 1989-90, Belgium experienced a wave of reported UFO sightings, with thousands of people claiming to see large, silent, low-flying black triangles.

☐ The Rendlesham Forest Incident: In 1980, U.S. Air Force personnel stationed in England reported seeing strange lights and an alleged spacecraft landing in Rendlesham Forest.

☐ Pilot UFO Encounters: Commercial and military pilots have reported numerous UFO encounters, with some instances recorded on radar and video.

☐ Ancient Astronaut Theories: Some believe that ancient art and texts provide evidence of ancient UFO sightings and extraterrestrial visitations.

☐ The Lubbock Lights: In 1951, a V-shaped formation of lights was observed over Lubbock, Texas, and photographed, becoming one of the most famous UFO sightings.

- ☐ UFOs in Ancient Art: Some medieval and renaissance paintings depict strange objects in the sky, resembling modern depictions of UFOs.

- ☐ FBI's UFO Files: The FBI has a publicly available online archive called "The Vault," which includes documents related to UFO investigations.

- ☐ Crop Circles: Some associate crop circles with UFO landings, though many have been proven to be made by humans.

- ☐ UFOs and Nuclear Facilities: Numerous reports exist of UFO sightings near nuclear power plants, missile sites, and other sensitive military facilities.

- ☐ The Hill Abduction: Betty and Barney Hill claimed to be abducted by aliens in 1961 in New Hampshire, making it one of the first widely publicized alien abduction stories.

- ☐ The "Wow!" Signal: In 1977, a strong narrowband radio signal was detected by astronomer Jerry R. Ehman while working on a SETI project, which he famously annotated with "Wow!"

- ☐ Fast Radio Bursts (FRBs): These high-energy astrophysical phenomena of unknown origin have sparked theories about advanced extraterrestrial civilizations.

- ☐ The Disclosure Project: This initiative, led by Dr. Steven Greer, aims to disclose alleged government information about UFOs and extraterrestrial life.

- ☐ Area 51: The U.S. military base in Nevada, known as Area 51, is a focal point of many UFO theories, often alleged to be a site for alien technology research.

Pirates and Adventures

☐ Pirate Codes: Pirates had their own code of conduct. The rules included how to divide loot and punishments for theft or cowardice.

☐ Blackbeard's Fearsome Appearance: The infamous pirate Blackbeard would light fuses in his beard during battles to create a fearsome, fiery appearance.

☐ Women Pirates: Anne Bonny and Mary Read were two of the most famous female pirates. They were as fierce as their male counterparts and feared across the seas.

☐ Pirate Democracy: Pirate ships often operated as democracies, with captains being elected by the crew and decisions made collectively.

☐ Walking the Plank: The act of walking the plank is mostly a myth popularized by books and movies. There's little historical evidence to suggest it was a common practice.

☐ The Jolly Roger: The skull and crossbones flag, known as the Jolly Roger, was used by pirates to intimidate their victims into surrendering without a fight.

☐ Pirate Treasure Maps: The stereotypical X marking the spot on a treasure map is more fiction than fact. Pirates typically divided their plunder rather than burying it.

☐ The Golden Age of Piracy: The period between 1650 and 1730 is known as the Golden Age of Piracy, when pirate activity was at its peak.

☐ Pirates and Parrots: The image of pirates with parrots comes from their journeys through exotic lands, where they encountered and sometimes captured these colorful birds.

☐ Real Pirate Ships: Contrary to popular belief, most pirate ships were small and fast, designed for quick attacks and easy escapes.

☐ Pirate Havens: Port Royal in Jamaica and Nassau in the Bahamas were known as pirate havens where pirates could rest and resupply.

☐ The Pirate Round: This was a sea route followed by pirates to rob ships laden with goods from the East Indies and the Indian Ocean.

☐ Pirate Speak: The pirate accent often depicted in movies is based on actor Robert Newton's portrayal of Long John Silver in the 1950 film "Treasure Island."

☐ Notorious Pirate Flags: Each pirate captain had a unique flag. Blackbeard's flag, for example, depicted a skeleton toasting the devil.

☐ The Barbarossa Brothers: The Barbarossa brothers were feared pirates in the Mediterranean. They later became admirals in the Ottoman Empire's fleet.

☐ Pirate Medicine: Pirate ships often had their own form of rough medicine. Amputations and crude surgeries were common after battles.

☐ The Pirate's Life Expectancy: Life as a pirate was harsh and dangerous. Many pirates didn't live past their late 20s.

- ☐ Calico Jack's Rackham's Design: The famous pirate Calico Jack Rackham designed the skull and crossed swords version of the Jolly Roger flag.

- ☐ Privateers: Privateers were pirates sanctioned by governments to attack and rob enemy ships during wartime.

- ☐ Pirate Loot: Contrary to popular belief, pirates often preferred to steal cargo like silk, spices, and rum rather than gold and silver.

Ancient Structures

- ☐ Great Pyramid of Giza: The Great Pyramid of Giza, built around 2560 BC, was the tallest man-made structure for over 3,800 years. It consists of approximately 2.3 million stone blocks.

- ☐ Stonehenge Mysteries: Stonehenge in England was constructed from 3000 BC to 2000 BC. Its stones were transported from over 200 miles away, and its exact purpose remains a mystery.

- ☐ The Colosseum's Grandeur: Rome's Colosseum, built in 80 AD, could seat around 50,000 spectators. It featured a retractable roof and was used for gladiator contests and public spectacles.

- ☐ Machu Picchu's Inca Ingenuity: Machu Picchu, an Incan city set high in the Andes Mountains, was built in the 15th century and remained hidden from the outside world until 1911.

- ☐ The Hanging Gardens of Babylon: One of the Seven Wonders of the Ancient World, the Hanging Gardens were said to be built in Babylon in the 6th century BC, but their existence remains unproven.

☐ The Great Wall of China's Length: The Great Wall of China stretches over 13,000 miles and was built over several centuries to protect against invasions.

☐ Petra's Rock Architecture: Petra, an ancient city in Jordan, is famous for its rock-cut architecture and water conduit system. It was carved directly into vibrant red, white, pink, and sandstone cliff faces.

☐ The Terracotta Army: The Terracotta Army, a collection of terracotta sculptures depicting the armies of Qin Shi Huang, the first Emperor of China, includes over 8,000 soldiers, 130 chariots, and 670 horses.

☐ The Lighthouse of Alexandria: Another Wonder of the Ancient World, the Lighthouse of Alexandria was built in the 3rd century BC and stood over 330 feet tall, guiding sailors safely to the harbor.

☐ Ancient Mayan Temples: The ancient Mayans built impressive temples and pyramids, like those found in Tikal, Guatemala. These structures were often aligned with astronomical events.

☐ Easter Island's Moai: The Moai are massive stone statues on Easter Island believed to have been carved by the Rapa Nui people between 1250 and 1500 AD.

☐ The Roman Aqueducts: The Romans built impressive aqueducts throughout their empire to supply water to urban centers. Some, like the Pont du Gard in France, still stand today.

☐ Angkor Wat's Grand Scale: Angkor Wat in Cambodia is the largest religious monument in the world, originally constructed as a Hindu temple in the early 12th century.

- [ ] The Parthenon's Perfection: The Parthenon in Athens, built in 447 BC, is a symbol of Ancient Greece and represents an ideal of architectural perfection.

- [ ] The Sphinx's Riddle: The Great Sphinx of Giza, with the body of a lion and the head of a human, is one of the largest and oldest statues in the world, but its exact origin and purpose are still unknown.

- [ ] Teotihuacan's Avenue of the Dead: The ancient Mesoamerican city of Teotihuacan features a central road called the Avenue of the Dead, flanked by impressive pyramids and structures.

- [ ] Knossos Palace's Labyrinth: The Palace of Knossos on Crete is associated with the myth of the Minotaur's labyrinth and was an advanced structure with sophisticated architecture.

- [ ] The Elgin Marbles Controversy: The Elgin Marbles, originally part of the Parthenon, were removed and taken to Britain in the early 19th century, leading to ongoing debates about cultural heritage.

- [ ] The Agra Fort's Majesty: Agra Fort in India was the main residence of the emperors of the Mughal Dynasty until 1638. It is a UNESCO World Heritage site.

- [ ] Borobudur's Buddhist Symbolism: Borobudur, in Central Java, Indonesia, is the world's largest Buddhist temple, decorated with 2,672 relief panels and 504 Buddha statues.

Mysterious Civilizations

- [ ] The Lost City of Atlantis: Atlantis is a legendary island first mentioned by Plato. It was said to be a technologically advanced utopian civilization that disappeared into the sea.

- [ ] The Sumerians' Writing: The Sumerians, one of the world's first civilizations in Mesopotamia, invented cuneiform, one of the earliest known writing systems, around 3500 BC.

- [ ] Easter Island's Moai Statues: Over 900 giant stone statues called Moai are found on Easter Island. They were carved by the Rapa Nui people, but how they transported these massive statues remains a mystery.

- [ ] The Nazca Lines: In Peru, the Nazca culture left behind enormous geoglyphs in the desert, known as the Nazca Lines, whose purpose is still debated, with theories ranging from religious to astronomical.

- [ ] The Minoan Civilization: The Minoans, living on the island of Crete, were known for their magnificent palaces, elaborate drainage systems, and the myth of the Minotaur in the labyrinth.

- [ ] The Indus Valley Civilization: This ancient civilization had advanced urban planning, including well-laid streets, drainage systems, and even public baths, but its script remains undeciphered.

- [ ] The Anasazi of Chaco Canyon: The Anasazi, or Ancestral Puebloans, built impressive cliff dwellings in Chaco Canyon, New Mexico, but mysteriously abandoned them in the 13th century.

- [ ] Göbekli Tepe's Age: Göbekli Tepe in Turkey is one of the oldest religious structures known, dating back to the 10th millennium BC, predating Stonehenge by 6,000 years.

- ☐ The Maya's Astronomical Knowledge: The Maya civilization had advanced knowledge of astronomy and mathematics, evident in their complex calendar systems.

- ☐ The Terracotta Army: China's first emperor, Qin Shi Huang, was buried with an army of life-sized terracotta soldiers, each with unique facial features.

- ☐ Angkor Wat's Grandeur: Angkor Wat in Cambodia is the largest religious monument in the world, originally a Hindu temple that transformed into a Buddhist one.

- ☐ The Mystery of the Olmecs: The Olmecs of Mesoamerica, known for their colossal head sculptures, had significant influence on later cultures but left little evidence about their society.

- ☐ The Lost City of Zerzura: Mentioned in Arabian folklore, Zerzura was a city of white marble hidden in the Sahara Desert, said to be full of treasures and guarded by black giants.

- ☐ Machu Picchu's Purpose: Built by the Incas, Machu Picchu's purpose remains a topic of debate, whether it was a royal estate, religious site, or a strategic military outpost.

- ☐ The Viking Settlements in America: Before Columbus, the Vikings had settlements in North America, known as Vinland, evidenced by the archaeological site at L'Anse aux Meadows.

- ☐ The Harappan Civilization's Script: The script of the Harappan Civilization, part of the Indus Valley Civilization, consists of about 400 symbols and has not been deciphered.

☐ The Mystery of Teotihuacan: The ancient city of Teotihuacan in Mexico, known for its vast Pyramid of the Sun, was one of the largest cities in the world but its builders remain unknown.

☐ The Dogon and Sirius B: The Dogon people in Mali have ancient astronomical knowledge about Sirius B, a companion star to Sirius, which they claim was given to them by extraterrestrial visitors.

☐ The Phaistos Disc: Discovered in Crete, the Phaistos Disc is made of fired clay and features a sequence of symbols that are still undeciphered.

☐ Troy's Reality and Myth: The city of Troy, famous from Homer's "Iliad," was long considered mythical until archaeological discoveries in modern Turkey revealed its historical basis.

Kings and Queens

☐ King Arthur and the Round Table: King Arthur, a legendary British leader, is known for his Knights of the Round Table and the quest for the Holy Grail. His existence, blending history and mythology, remains debated.

☐ Queen Cleopatra's Intelligence: Cleopatra, the last active ruler of the Ptolemaic Kingdom of Egypt, was known for her intelligence, speaking several languages, and being a shrewd politician.

☐ Genghis Khan's Empire: Genghis Khan founded the Mongol Empire, the largest contiguous empire in history, covering vast parts of Asia and extending into Europe.

☐ King Tutankhamun's Tomb: The Egyptian Pharaoh Tutankhamun, or King Tut, became famous after his nearly intact tomb was discovered in 1922, sparking global interest in ancient Egypt.

- [ ] Queen Elizabeth I's Reign: Known as the Virgin Queen, Elizabeth I ruled England during its "Golden Age," promoting the arts, exploration, and the Protestant religion.

- [ ] Charlemagne's Vast Empire: Charlemagne, or Charles the Great, was King of the Franks and Lombards and later became the first Holy Roman Emperor, uniting much of western and central Europe.

- [ ] King Louis XIV's Long Reign: Louis XIV of France, known as the Sun King, had the longest recorded reign of any monarch of a sovereign country, ruling for 72 years.

- [ ] Emperor Qin Shi Huang's Terracotta Army: The first Emperor of China, Qin Shi Huang, is known for unifying China and for the Terracotta Army that guards his tomb.

- [ ] Alexander the Great's Conquests: By the age of 30, Alexander the Great had created one of the largest empires in history, stretching from Greece to northwestern India.

- [ ] Queen Victoria's Era: Queen Victoria's reign, known as the Victorian era, was a period of industrial, cultural, political, and military change in the United Kingdom.

- [ ] King Richard the Lionheart: A central figure in the Crusades, Richard I of England was known for his courage and prowess in battle, earning him the name Lionheart.

☐ The Madness of King George III: King George III of England is known for his bouts of madness, later believed to be a symptom of the genetic disease porphyria.

☐ Empress Wu Zetian's Rule: Wu Zetian was the only female emperor in the history of China, known for her effective and ambitious rule in the Tang dynasty.

☐ Henry VIII's Six Wives: King Henry VIII of England is famous for having six wives and for his role in the separation of the Church of England from the Roman Catholic Church.

☐ Catherine the Great's Modernization of Russia: Catherine II, known as Catherine the Great, expanded Russian territories and promoted the modernization and westernization of Russia.

☐ King Solomon's Wisdom: Solomon, a king of Israel and a figure in Jewish, Christian, and Islamic traditions, was known for his wisdom, wealth, and building projects, including the First Temple in Jerusalem.

☐ Emperor Nero's Infamy: Nero, a Roman Emperor, is infamous for his tyrannical rule, and according to popular belief, he played the fiddle while Rome burned, although this is historically disputed.

☐ The Legend of Queen Boudica: Boudica, a queen of the British Celtic Iceni tribe, led an uprising against the occupying forces of the Roman Empire in AD 60–61.

☐ King Leonidas' Stand at Thermopylae: Leonidas I was a warrior king of the Greek city-state of Sparta and is most famous for his heroic stand against the Persian army at the Battle of Thermopylae.

- [ ] Pharaoh Ramses II's Monuments: Ramses II, also known as Ramses the Great, was one of Egypt's most powerful and celebrated pharaohs, known for his extensive building programs and for fathering over 100 children.

Lost Artifacts

- [ ] The Amber Room: Once considered the "Eighth Wonder of the World," the Amber Room in Russia, made entirely of amber and gold, was looted during World War II and has never been recovered.

- [ ] Lost Fabergé Eggs: Of the 50 Imperial Fabergé Eggs created for the Russian Royal Family, eight are missing, their whereabouts a mystery since the Russian Revolution.

- [ ] The Honjo Masamune Sword: A symbol of the Shogun's power in Japan, this legendary samurai sword, created by a famous swordsmith, was lost after World War II.

- [ ] The Ark of the Covenant: Described in the Bible as containing the Ten Commandments, the Ark of the Covenant's location has been a subject of fascination and speculation for centuries.

- [ ] The Lost Library of the Maya: The Spanish conquest of the Yucatán Peninsula led to the destruction of most of the Mayan codices, with only a few surviving, leaving much of Mayan history and knowledge lost.

- [ ] King John's Lost Treasure: In 1216, England's King John lost his crown jewels and other precious artifacts in The Wash, a bay in Eastern England, and they have never been found.

- [ ] Montezuma's Treasure: Legend says that a vast treasure of gold and jewels, belonging to Aztec emperor Montezuma, was hidden from the Spanish conquistadors and remains undiscovered.

- [ ] The Lost Dutchman's Gold Mine: Said to be located in the Superstition Mountains of Arizona, this mine supposedly holds a vast amount of gold, but its exact location remains a mystery.

- [ ] The Patiala Necklace: This necklace, containing 2,930 diamonds including the world's seventh-largest diamond, the "De Beers," disappeared from the Royal Treasury of Patiala in 1948.

- [ ] The Irish Crown Jewels: Stolen in 1907 from Dublin Castle, the Irish Crown Jewels, which included star and badge regalia, have never been recovered.

- [ ] The Menorah from the Second Temple: Carried away by the Romans when they sacked Jerusalem in 70 AD, this golden Menorah's fate is unknown.

- [ ] The Florentine Diamond: A 137-carat yellow diamond of Indian origin, the Florentine Diamond disappeared after the Austrian royal family took it into exile in 1918.

- [ ] The Lost Romanov Jewels: Following the execution of the Russian royal family in 1918, many of their renowned jewels vanished, sparking numerous treasure hunts.

- [ ] The Tomb of Antony and Cleopatra: The tomb of the famous lovers, Antony and Cleopatra, remains undiscovered, with many believing it holds untold riches.

- [ ] The San Miguel & The 1715 Treasure Fleet: A Spanish fleet carrying gold, silver, and jewelry worth today's equivalent of hundreds of millions of dollars sank off the coast of Florida in 1715. Much of the treasure remains unfound.

- [ ] The Scepter of Dagobert: Part of the French Crown Jewels, this gold and cloisonné enamel scepter from the 7th century was stolen in 1795 and has never been recovered.

- [ ] The Peking Man Fossils: Discovered in China and dating back to around 500,000 years ago, these priceless Homo erectus fossils disappeared in 1941 during World War II.

- [ ] The Just Judges Panel: Part of the famous Ghent Altarpiece, this panel was stolen in 1934 from Saint Bavo's Cathedral, Ghent, and remains missing.

- [ ] The Imperial Seal of China: Carved in 221 BC, the Imperial Seal of China passed through various hands before disappearing in the chaos of war in the early 10th century.

- [ ] The Mahogany Ship: Legend speaks of a 16th-century Portuguese shipwreck buried in the sands near Warrnambool, Australia. If found, it could rewrite the history of European exploration of Australia.

Funny Laws of Countries

- [ ] Chewing Gum in Singapore: Selling or importing chewing gum in Singapore is illegal, a law put in place to keep public spaces clean.

- [ ] No Camouflage in Barbados: In Barbados, it's illegal for anyone, including children, to wear camouflage clothing. This law is to prevent confusion with military personnel.

- ☐ Silent in Switzerland: In Switzerland, it's illegal to flush the toilet after 10 pm in an apartment building, as it's considered noise pollution.

- ☐ A Ban on Winnie the Pooh in Poland: In a small town in Poland, Winnie the Pooh was banned from a playground because he doesn't wear pants!

- ☐ No Salmon Suspicion in England: Under the Salmon Act of 1986, it's illegal in England to handle salmon in suspicious circumstances.

- ☐ Ban on Haggis in the U.S.: Traditional Scottish haggis has been banned in the U.S. since 1971 because it contains sheep's lung, an ingredient not allowed in food.

- ☐ No Public Kissing in Dubai: Public displays of affection, including kissing, are strictly prohibited in Dubai and can result in fines or even jail time.

- ☐ Whale Ownership in the U.K.: In the U.K., it's a law that any whale or sturgeon found on the coast belongs to the monarch.

- ☐ No Heels in Greece: It's illegal to wear high heels at ancient archaeological sites in Greece to prevent damage.

- ☐ Flying Saucer Fines in France: In the town of Chateauneuf-du-Pape, France, it's illegal to fly a flying saucer, and you can be fined if you land one there.

- ☐ Ban on Durian in Public Transport: In countries like Singapore and Thailand, carrying a durian fruit on public transport is banned due to its strong smell.

- ☐ No Dying in Parliament: It's illegal to die in the Houses of Parliament in England because it's a Royal Palace.

- ☐ Piano Restrictions in Japan: In Japan, you must keep your piano playing to a minimum to avoid disturbing the neighbors.

- ☐ No Running Out of Gas in Germany: On the autobahn in Germany, it's illegal to run out of gas, as stopping for preventable reasons is not allowed.

- ☐ Lollipop Ban in Washington: In the city of Spokane, Washington, the U.S., lollipops are banned. Hard candies are okay, though!

- ☐ No Dirty Cars in Russia: In Moscow, driving a dirty car is considered an offense and can attract a fine.

- ☐ No Reincarnation Without Permission: In China, Buddhist monks must have permission from the government to reincarnate.

- ☐ Name Restrictions in Denmark: Parents in Denmark must choose their baby's name from a pre-approved list of 7,000 names.

- ☐ Ban on Bear Wrestling: In Alabama, USA, bear wrestling matches are illegal.

- ☐ Giant Monster Law in Washington: In Washington, it's illegal to harass Bigfoot or other undiscovered species, so monster hunting is off-limits!

Unusual Political Traditions

- ☐ The Queen's Speech in the UK: Every year, the Queen of England delivers a speech to open Parliament.

Interestingly, the speech is written by the government and outlines its agenda.

☐ Swearing-In on a Giant Bible in the U.S.: U.S. Presidents often swear in on a giant Bible during their inauguration. George Washington started this tradition in 1789.

☐ Bhutan's Gross National Happiness: In Bhutan, the government measures the country's success through "Gross National Happiness" instead of Gross Domestic Product (GDP), prioritizing the well-being of its citizens.

☐ The Black Rod Ceremony in the UK: In a British parliamentary tradition, the doors to the House of Commons are slammed in the face of the Black Rod, a senior officer, symbolizing the Commons' independence from the monarchy.

☐ Papal Conclave's White Smoke: When a new Pope is chosen in Vatican City, white smoke is released from the Sistine Chapel chimney, signaling to the world the successful election.

☐ Iceland's Open-Air Parliament: The Althing, one of the world's oldest parliaments, originally met outdoors in a place called Thingvellir in Iceland, starting around AD 930.

☐ Poland's First Lady Tradition: In Poland, the First Lady has her own office and responsibilities, often focusing on charitable and cultural affairs.

☐ New Zealand's Haka in Parliament: New Zealand politicians have been known to perform the traditional Maori haka, a ceremonial dance or challenge, in parliament.

- ☐ The 'Well of Death' in India's Parliament: The area in front of the Lok Sabha (House of the People) speaker's podium is colloquially known as the 'Well of Death' due to the intensity of debates there.

- ☐ No Applause in the Japanese Diet: In Japan's parliament, or Diet, clapping is not allowed. Instead, members express approval by saying "Agreed."

- ☐ San Marino's Dual Leadership: San Marino, one of the world's smallest countries, has two heads of state called Captains Regent, elected every six months.

- ☐ Sword and Mace in Canada's Parliament: A sword and mace are carried into the Canadian Senate before each session, symbolizing the authority of the Queen and the Parliament.

- ☐ Tonga's Royal Kava Ceremony: In Tonga, a kava ceremony involving a traditional Polynesian drink is performed during important state occasions.

- ☐ France's Co-Prince of Andorra: The President of France also serves as a Co-Prince of Andorra, a small principality between France and Spain, sharing the role with the Bishop of Urgell.

- ☐ The Netherlands' Prinsjesdag: On Prinsjesdag, the Dutch monarch rides in a golden carriage to Parliament to read a speech outlining the government's plan for the year.

- ☐ Italy's 'Cursing' Lawmakers: In Italy's Parliament, it's not uncommon for lawmakers to use strong language and even hand gestures during heated debates.

- ☐ Sri Lanka's Astrology in Politics: Astrology plays a significant role in Sri Lankan politics, with many politicians consulting astrologers for auspicious dates to hold elections or take office.

- [ ] South Korea's Filibuster Record: In South Korea, one lawmaker set a record by speaking for more than 12 hours in a filibuster, using lengthy speeches to delay legislation.

- [ ] Palau's Traditional Chiefs in Politics: In Palau, traditional chiefs play a role in government, advising on cultural and traditional matters.

- [ ] No Talking in the Eritrean Assembly: Eritrea's National Assembly has a unique rule where members cannot talk inside the hall. They must write down their questions and comments.

Fun Facts About Politicians

- [ ] Winston Churchill's Parrot: British Prime Minister Winston Churchill had a parrot named Charlie, who was known for mimicking Churchill and allegedly lived to be over 100 years old.

- [ ] Queen Elizabeth II's Many Animals: Queen Elizabeth II has owned more than 30 corgis during her reign, along with numerous other animals, including an elephant, jaguars, and sloths, given as gifts from other countries.

- [ ] Andrew Jackson's Cheese Party: U.S. President Andrew Jackson once had a 1,400-pound block of cheese in the White House. He invited the public to help eat it, leading to a massive cheese party.

- [ ] Theodore Roosevelt's Menagerie: President Roosevelt had a collection of pets at the White House, including a bear, a badger, snakes, dogs, cats, and a one-legged rooster.

☐ Julius Caesar's Fear of Cats: The great Roman leader Julius Caesar was rumored to have a fear of cats, known as Ailurophobia.

☐ Grover Cleveland's Wedding in the White House: U.S. President Grover Cleveland is the only president to have had a wedding in the White House.

☐ Caligula's Horse as a Consul: Roman Emperor Caligula is said to have loved his horse Incitatus so much that he gave it a house and even planned to make it a consul.

☐ Lyndon B. Johnson's Amphibious Car: U.S. President Lyndon B. Johnson owned an amphibious car and would scare his guests by driving into a lake, pretending the brakes had failed.

☐ Kim Jong-il's Golf Skills: North Korean leader Kim Jong-il reportedly claimed to have scored 11 holes-in-one in a single round of golf.

☐ Richard Nixon's Bowling Alley: President Nixon was an avid bowler and had a one-lane bowling alley installed in the White House.

☐ Vladimir Putin's Black Belt: Russian President Vladimir Putin holds a black belt in judo and has co-authored a book on the subject.

☐ Benjamin Franklin's Musical Invention: Founding Father Benjamin Franklin invented a musical instrument called the glass armonica, which Mozart and Beethoven composed music for.

☐ Queen Victoria's Secret Code: Queen Victoria and Prince Albert communicated in a secret code in their letters to each other.

- Barack Obama's Comic Book Collection: Former U.S. President Barack Obama is a collector of Spider-Man and Conan the Barbarian comic books.

- Genghis Khan's Identity Protection: Mongolian ruler Genghis Khan was so protective of his identity that no paintings or sculptures of him were made during his lifetime.

- Margaret Thatcher's Ice Cream Chemistry: Before her political career, British Prime Minister Margaret Thatcher was a research chemist who helped develop the soft-serve ice cream process.

- Fidel Castro's Dairy Obsession: Cuban leader Fidel Castro loved dairy so much that he tried to breed super cows and once consumed 18 scoops of ice cream in one sitting.

- John Quincy Adams' Morning Routine: U.S. President John Quincy Adams regularly went skinny-dipping in the Potomac River as part of his morning routine.

- Nelson Mandela's Cameo in a Movie: South African President Nelson Mandela made a cameo as a schoolteacher reciting his own speech in the 1992 film "Malcolm X."

- The Royal Penguin Knight: In 2008, a king penguin named Nils Olav was knighted at Edinburgh Zoo in Scotland and is considered a member of the Norwegian King's Guard.

Government Buildings

- The White House, USA: The White House, home and office of the U.S. President, was designed by Irish-born architect James Hoban and has been the residence of every U.S. president since John Adams in 1800.

- [ ] The Lotus Temple, India: While not a government building, the Lotus Temple in Delhi, known for its stunning lotus flower design, is a Bahá'í House of Worship promoting unity.

- [ ] The Pentagon, USA: The Pentagon, the world's largest office building, is the headquarters of the U.S. Department of Defense and has twice the floor space of the Empire State Building.

- [ ] The Kremlin, Russia: The Kremlin in Moscow, a historic fortified complex, includes five palaces, four cathedrals, and serves as the official residence of the President of Russia.

- [ ] The Beehive, New Zealand: New Zealand's parliamentary executive wing building is known as the Beehive due to its unique shape. It was designed by Scottish architect Sir Basil Spence.

- [ ] Palace of Westminster, UK: The Palace of Westminster houses the two houses of the Parliament of the UK. Its iconic clock tower, Big Ben, is often mistakenly thought to be the name of the clock.

- [ ] The Royal Palace of Amsterdam, Netherlands: Originally built as a city hall during the Dutch Golden Age, it later became the royal palace for King Louis Napoleon and subsequent Dutch monarchs.

- [ ] The Forbidden City, China: The Forbidden City in Beijing was the Chinese imperial palace for almost 500 years. It's called forbidden because no one could enter or leave without the emperor's permission.

- [ ] Château de Versailles, France: The Palace of Versailles, a symbol of the absolute monarchy of the

Ancien Régime, was the principal royal residence of France from 1682 until the start of the French Revolution.

☐ The Hungarian Parliament Building: In Budapest, this Gothic Revival-style building is one of Europe's oldest legislative buildings and is notable for its detailed architecture and the Holy Crown of Hungary.

☐ Hundertwasserhaus, Austria: Not a government building but a remarkable apartment complex in Vienna, designed by artist Friedensreich Hundertwasser, known for its colorful and uneven floors.

☐ The Sultan Omar Ali Saifuddien Mosque, Brunei: A major landmark and Islamic symbol in Brunei, the mosque features a golden dome and an interior of Italian marble walls, chandeliers, and stained glass windows.

☐ The Parliament House of Australia: Located in Canberra, it's known for its modern, boomerang-like design and features a grass-covered roof, symbolizing the building rising from the landscape.

☐ The Scottish Parliament Building: Opened in 2004 in Edinburgh, this building is famous for its unconventional architectural style, which is intended to evoke the landscapes of Scotland.

☐ Reichstag Building, Germany: Known for its glass dome, the Reichstag is where the German parliament meets. The dome is designed to be environmentally friendly, providing light and ventilation.

☐ The Capitolio, Cuba: In Havana, the Capitolio was the seat of government in Cuba until the Cuban Revolution and is now home to the Cuban Academy of Sciences.

☐ Jatiya Sangsad Bhaban, Bangladesh: Designed by American architect Louis Kahn, the national parliament building in Dhaka is renowned for its geometric design and use of natural light.

☐ Palacio de Bellas Artes, Mexico: Not a government building but a prominent cultural center in Mexico City, it's known for its stunning architecture and murals by famous Mexican artists.

☐ Oslo Opera House, Norway: Resembling a glacier jutting into the Oslo fjord, this modern building is home to the Norwegian National Opera and Ballet.

☐ Musée du Louvre, France: Originally a royal palace, the Louvre in Paris is now the world's largest art museum and a historic monument, famous for its glass pyramid entrance.

Eccentric Money

☐ Island of Yap's Stone Money: On the Micronesian island of Yap, large stone disks called Rai stones were used as currency, some as large as 12 feet in diameter, making them probably the heaviest money in the world.

☐ Bitcoin, the Digital Currency: Bitcoin is a digital cryptocurrency with no physical form. Created in 2009, it's the first decentralized digital currency, meaning it works without a central bank or administrator.

☐ The Tally Sticks of Medieval England: In medieval England, wooden sticks known as tally sticks were used as currency. They were split into halves to record debts, with each party keeping a half.

☐ Zimbabwe's Hyperinflation Money: In 2008, Zimbabwe experienced such severe hyperinflation that they issued a 100 trillion Zimbabwean dollar note, one of the highest denominations of currency ever printed.

☐ Cocoa Beans in Ancient Maya: The ancient Mayans used cocoa beans as currency. These beans were so valuable that they were often counterfeited by filling empty cocoa bean shells with dirt.

☐ Canada's Glow-in-the-Dark Coin: In 2017, Canada released the world's first glow-in-the-dark coin in circulation. It features the Northern Lights and glows in the dark.

☐ Dutch Guilder's Snip: The Dutch 1,000 Guilder note, known as the "Snip," featured a large, colorful bird and was one of the most artistic and vibrant banknotes.

☐ Tea Bricks in Siberia and Mongolia: In some regions of Siberia and Mongolia, tea bricks (compressed blocks of tea leaves) were used as currency until the 20th century.

☐ Squirrel Pelts in Medieval Finland: In medieval Finland, squirrel pelts were used as currency, and there were even standard rates for different parts of the squirrel.

☐ Australia's Polymer Banknotes: Australia was the first country to introduce polymer (plastic) banknotes in 1988, which are more durable and secure than paper notes.

☐ Salt as Ancient Currency: Salt was so valuable in ancient times that it was used as currency. The word "salary" even comes from "sal," the Latin word for salt.

☐ Nauru's Oddly Shaped Coins: The tiny island nation of Nauru issued star-shaped and triangular coins, making their currency unique in shape and design.

☐ The Seven-Sided Coin of Britain: The British 50 pence coin is heptagonal, making it the world's first seven-sided coin when it was introduced in 1969.

☐ Norway's Hole-in-the-Center Coin: Norway once issued a 50 Øre coin that had a hole in the center. It was in circulation until the denomination was discontinued in 2012.

☐ The Tongan Pa'anga: In Tonga, one of their currencies is the Pa'anga, which features colorful and intricate designs, including pictures of the royal family.

☐ The Cook Islands' Sea Creatures Coins: The Cook Islands have currency featuring sea creatures. Some coins even have a real pearl embedded in them.

☐ Somalia's Guitar-Shaped Coins: Somalia issued guitar-shaped coins, a unique and unconventional design for currency.

☐ Bhutan's Vertical Banknotes: Bhutan released vertical banknotes, a rare orientation for currency, showcasing their unique cultural heritage and landmarks.

☐ The Giant Rai of Micronesia: In Micronesia, giant stone discs, some weighing several tons, were used as currency and are still exchanged in traditional rituals.

☐ Peru's Sol Coin with a Puzzle: Peru issued a series of coins called "Wealth and Pride of Peru," each highlighting a different cultural or natural resource.

When placed together, the coins form an image of
the Tumi, an ancient ceremonial knife.

Economic Explorations

- [ ] Sweden's Negative Interest Rates: In 2015, Sweden's central bank adopted negative interest rates, meaning banks were charged for keeping money, encouraging them to lend more.

- [ ] The Tulip Mania: In the 17th century in the Netherlands, tulip bulbs became so expensive that they were used as currency and traded like stocks. This was one of the first recorded financial bubbles.

- [ ] India's Demonetization: In 2016, India suddenly declared that 500 and 1,000 rupee notes were no longer legal tender to combat corruption and counterfeit currency, leading to a massive economic upheaval.

- [ ] The Zimbabwean Hyperinflation: In 2008, Zimbabwe experienced hyperinflation so severe that prices would double every 24 hours, leading to the issuance of a 100 trillion Zimbabwean dollar note.

- [ ] Ithaca HOURS: In Ithaca, New York, there's a local currency called "HOURS," which is earned by doing community work and can be spent at local businesses.

- [ ] The Big Mac Index: The Economist magazine uses the price of a McDonald's Big Mac in different countries to measure purchasing power parity, calling it the Big Mac Index.

- [ ] The Island of Stone Money: The Pacific island of Yap uses large stone disks called Rai as money. Some are too large to move and are exchanged verbally.

☐ Cuba's Dual Currency: Until 2021, Cuba had two currencies: one for locals (CUP) and one for tourists (CUC), with different values and uses.

☐ The Great Emu War and Economy: In 1932, Australia faced an agricultural economic threat from emus, leading to the bizarre "Great Emu War" where soldiers were deployed to control the emu population.

☐ Free Money Experiment in Canada: In the 1970s, the town of Dauphin, Canada, conducted an experiment where residents were guaranteed a minimum income, resulting in improved health and education outcomes.

☐ Potato Bonds in Russia: In 1998, after an economic crisis, the Russian region of Udmurtia issued bonds that could be redeemed for potatoes, literally making potatoes a form of currency.

☐ The Billion Dollar Coin Idea: During the 2013 U.S. debt ceiling crisis, there was a proposal to mint a trillion-dollar platinum coin to avert a government default.

☐ Iceland's Fish Currency: After World War II, Iceland used fish as its primary export and base of economy, leading to the term "fish currency" for its economy's reliance on fish.

☐ The Dotcom Bubble: In the late 1990s and early 2000s, the dotcom bubble saw the rise and fall of numerous internet-based companies, with their stock prices skyrocketing then rapidly declining.

☐ Wörgl's Experiment with Free Money: In 1932, the Austrian town of Wörgl introduced a local currency with a negative interest rate to stimulate the economy during the Great Depression, and it worked successfully for a short period.

- [ ] The Use of Cowry Shells: Cowry shells were used as currency in various parts of the world, including Africa and Asia, for centuries.

- [ ] Brazil's Real Plan: In 1994, Brazil successfully stabilized its economy with the "Real Plan," which involved introducing a new currency, the Real, and was unusual in its approach to tackling hyperinflation.

- [ ] The Mississippi Bubble: In 18th century France, the Mississippi Bubble was a financial scheme that led to rampant speculation and a disastrous economic collapse.

- [ ] The Birth of PayPal: PayPal started as a cryptography company and evolved into a global online payment system, revolutionizing digital transactions.

- [ ] Monopoly's Teaching Origin: The board game Monopoly was originally created to teach the economic theory of single-tax and demonstrate the negatives of concentrating land in private monopolies.

Rich & Funny

- [ ] Mansa Musa's Riches: Mansa Musa, the 14th-century emperor of Mali, is considered the richest person in history. His wealth was so immense that during his pilgrimage to Mecca, he distributed so much gold that it caused inflation in the regions he passed through.

- [ ] The Rothschilds' Pigeons: The Rothschild family, known for their banking empire, used carrier pigeons to relay financial information, giving them an edge in early international finance.

☐ Queen Elizabeth II's Swan Ownership: In the UK, all unmarked mute swans on open waters are considered property of the Crown. Queen Elizabeth II technically owns all such swans in England.

☐ John D. Rockefeller's Wealth: John D. Rockefeller, the American oil magnate, was so wealthy that his fortune was worth nearly 2% of the total U.S. economy at its peak.

☐ The Sultan of Brunei's Car Collection: The Sultan of Brunei is said to own one of the largest private car collections in the world, with over 7,000 cars including custom-made Ferraris and Rolls-Royces.

☐ Andrew Carnegie's Libraries: Andrew Carnegie, a wealthy industrialist, donated much of his fortune to establish public libraries across the United States, United Kingdom, and other countries.

☐ Cleopatra's Pearl: Cleopatra, the last active ruler of the Ptolemaic Kingdom of Egypt, reportedly dissolved a pearl in a glass of vinegar and drank it to win a wager with Marc Antony that she could consume the wealth of an entire nation in one meal.

☐ Nicholas II's Fabergé Eggs: Tsar Nicholas II of Russia commissioned the creation of Fabergé Eggs, some of the most expensive and exquisite pieces of art, as Easter gifts for his wife.

☐ Bill Gates' Time Value: At one point, it was calculated that for Bill Gates, picking up a $100 bill from the ground would be a waste of his time, considering how much he earns per second.

- [ ] The First Billionaire: John D. Rockefeller was the world's first confirmed U.S. dollar billionaire.

- [ ] Warren Buffett's Frugality: Warren Buffett, one of the richest men in the world, is known for his frugal lifestyle, including living in the same house he bought in 1958 for $31,500.

- [ ] The Lost Treasure of Lima: In the 1820s, a vast fortune from Lima, Peru, was supposedly buried on Cocos Island. It has never been found despite numerous expeditions.

- [ ] J.K. Rowling's Billionaire Status: J.K. Rowling, author of the Harry Potter series, became the world's first billionaire author but lost her billionaire status because of her extensive charitable giving.

- [ ] Elon Musk's Space Ambitions: Elon Musk, founder of SpaceX, aims to colonize Mars and even plans to send paying customers around the moon.

- [ ] King Solomon's Wealth: According to the Bible, King Solomon was so wealthy that he made silver as common in Jerusalem as stones.

- [ ] Howard Hughes' Eccentricities: The wealthy American businessman Howard Hughes was known for his eccentric behavior, including designing a special bra for actress Jane Russell and obsessively watching movies in a dark room for days.

- [ ] The Getty Family Kidnapping: In 1973, John Paul Getty III, the grandson of oil tycoon J. Paul Getty, was kidnapped, but his grandfather initially refused to pay the ransom.

- [ ] The Wealth of the Medici Family: The Medici family, Italian bankers, and politicians were so wealthy and powerful that they produced four Popes and two queens of France.

☐ Oprah Winfrey's Success Story: Oprah Winfrey, one of the most successful women in the world, came from a poor background and built a media empire, becoming North America's first black multi-billionaire.

☐ Richard Branson's Private Island: Sir Richard Branson, the founder of Virgin Group, owns a private island called Necker Island, which he bought for $180,000 in 1978, and is now a luxury resort.

Unusual Taxes in History

☐ Window Tax: In England and France, a window tax was imposed in the 18th and 19th centuries. People bricked up their windows to avoid the tax, leading to some very dark homes!

☐ Beard Tax: Peter the Great of Russia imposed a tax on beards in the 18th century. He wanted to modernize Russian society and saw beards as old-fashioned.

☐ Salt Tax: In ancient China and medieval Europe, governments taxed salt – a valuable and essential commodity, leading to widespread smuggling.

☐ Hat Tax: In 1784, England introduced a tax on men's hats. Hat-wearers had to buy a stamp to stick inside their hat, and forging a hat stamp was a serious crime.

☐ Playing Card Tax: In the 16th century, England imposed a tax on playing cards, which is why the Ace of Spades often has a more elaborate design – it was used to display the tax stamp.

- ☐ Urine Tax: Ancient Roman Emperor Vespasian placed a tax on urine collected from public urinals, as it was used for various chemical processes, including tanning leather.

- ☐ Candle Tax: In England, a tax was imposed on candles in the 18th century. This led many people to go to bed early to avoid the expense of lighting their homes.

- ☐ Hearth Tax: In 1662, England and Scotland implemented a hearth tax, charging residents for each fireplace in their home. This often resulted in people bricking up their fireplaces.

- ☐ Soap Tax: England, in the 18th century, had a heavy tax on soap, considered a luxury item, which unfortunately discouraged cleanliness and hygiene.

- ☐ Powder Tax: In 1795, England introduced a tax on powdered wigs. This tax hastened the end of the fashion for wearing wigs.

- ☐ Sunshine Tax: In Spain, there's a tax on solar power, often humorously referred to as a tax on the sun.

- ☐ Bachelor Tax: In ancient Rome and some U.S. states in the early 20th century, single men were taxed more heavily than married ones, encouraging marriage.

- ☐ Royal Fart Tax: Roman Emperor Claudius allegedly imposed a tax on people who passed gas in the Roman baths, believing it was beneficial to one's health.

- ☐ Dancing Tax: In Germany, there's a tax on dancing. Clubs and venues hosting dance events are required to pay a culture tax.

- [ ] Wallpaper Tax: In 1712, England introduced a tax on printed wallpaper. People started hanging plain wallpaper and then hand-painting it to avoid the tax.

- [ ] Cow Flatulence Tax: Some countries have considered a tax on cow flatulence due to its contribution to greenhouse gas emissions.

- [ ] Blueberry Tax: In Maine, there's a specific tax for anyone growing, handling, processing, or selling blueberries.

- [ ] Jock Tax: Athletes in the U.S. sometimes face a "jock tax," where states and cities tax them for the income earned while playing in their jurisdiction.

- [ ] Swedish Baby Naming Tax: In Sweden, parents must pay a fine if they don't register their baby's name by the time the child is five months old.

- [ ] TV Detector Van Tax: In the UK, you need a license to watch live television broadcasts, and the government uses detector vans to find unlicensed TV watchers.

Fun Facts About Money

- [ ] Monopoly Money Printing: The amount of money printed yearly for the board game Monopoly is more than real money printed by the U.S. Treasury.

- [ ] Canada's Scratch-and-Sniff Money: Canadian $100 bills are rumored to smell like maple syrup when scratched, although the Canadian government denies any scent was intentionally added.

☐ ATMs and the Chocolate Bar: The world's first ATM was installed in London in 1967, but in the U.S., the first automated dispenser machine gave out chocolate bars, not cash.

☐ Sweden's Cashless Society: Sweden is so advanced in electronic payments that some banks don't handle cash at all, making it a nearly cashless society.

☐ The World's Smallest Currency: The smallest currency unit is the Iranian Rial, where 10,000 rials is roughly equivalent to 1 US dollar.

☐ The Yap Islands' Stone Money: On the Yap Islands in Micronesia, the largest stone money is 12 feet in diameter and was used for major transactions, despite being immovable.

☐ Zimbabwe's 100 Trillion Dollar Note: Zimbabwe once issued a 100 trillion Zimbabwean dollar note during a period of hyperinflation – it was not enough to buy a loaf of bread.

☐ Two-Dollar Bills in the U.S.: U.S. $2 bills are so rare that some people think they are counterfeit, but they are legal tender.

☐ J.S.G. Boggs' Art Money: Artist J.S.G. Boggs drew detailed replicas of U.S. banknotes and used them to buy goods and services as a form of art.

☐ Australia's Waterproof Money: Australia uses polymer banknotes which are waterproof and more durable than paper money.

☐ Currency with Braille: Some countries, including Canada and India, have banknotes with Braille-like markings for visually impaired individuals.

☐ North Korea's Counterfeiting: North Korea is known for producing "superdollars," counterfeit U.S. dollars so well made that they are hard to distinguish from the real thing.

☐ Disney Dollars: Disneyland and Walt Disney World once issued their own currency, Disney Dollars, which could be spent within the parks.

☐ Nixon's Giant Panda Loan: In 1972, President Nixon loaned China a million dollars. Instead of paying it back, China gave the U.S. two giant pandas.

☐ The Euro Notes' Fictional Bridges: The bridges on Euro notes are fictional designs representing different European architectural styles, not real bridges.

☐ Hungary's Hyperinflation: After World War II, Hungary experienced such severe hyperinflation that the value of its highest denomination, the 100 quintillion pengő note, almost doubled every 15 hours.

☐ Wooden Money in the U.S.: During the Great Depression, a town in Washington, U.S., issued wooden money due to a shortage of metal and paper currency.

☐ Bermuda's Hog Money: Bermuda's first currency in the early 17th century was called "hog money," featuring a pig on one side of the coins.

☐ Albert Einstein on Israeli Currency: Albert Einstein was once offered the presidency of Israel. He declined, but his face appeared on Israeli banknotes.

☐ Ancient China's Knife and Key Money: In ancient China, before coins, people used miniature replicas of knives and keys as money.

Unusual Workplaces

☐ Underwater Hotel Manager: At the underwater hotel in the Maldives, the manager oversees operations below the ocean's surface, ensuring guests have a unique and submerged experience.

☐ Professional Sleeper: Some people get paid to sleep as part of scientific research studies on sleep disorders or to test the comfort of beds and pillows in hotels.

☐ LEGO Sculptor: LEGO sculptors, or Master Builders, work at LEGOland to create amazing structures entirely out of LEGO bricks, turning a childhood pastime into a professional job.

☐ Water Slide Tester: Some lucky individuals work as water slide testers, traveling to different water parks to test the safety and fun level of the slides.

☐ Private Island Caretaker: In some exotic locations, caretakers are employed to look after private islands, ensuring they are well-maintained and ready for when the owners visit.

☐ Professional Panda Cuddler: In China, panda caretakers get to cuddle and care for baby pandas, helping in the conservation efforts for these adorable creatures.

☐ Ice Cream Flavor Guru: At companies like Ben & Jerry's, there are flavor gurus whose job is to invent new and delicious ice cream flavors.

☐ Bicycle Fisherman: In Amsterdam, there are bicycle fishermen who use magnets to pull out bicycles that have fallen into the city's canals.

- ☐ Professional Mermaid: Professional mermaids perform at events and in underwater shows, often wearing custom-made, intricately designed mermaid tails.

- ☐ Gumologist: A gumologist tests chewing gum for flavor, texture, and bubble-making capacity, making sure each piece is just right before it hits the shelves.

- ☐ Roller Coaster Engineer: These engineers design and test roller coasters, combining creativity with physics to ensure they are both thrilling and safe.

- ☐ Netflix Tagger: Netflix taggers watch shows and movies and tag them with specific keywords to help create accurate and personalized recommendations for users.

- ☐ Fortune Cookie Writer: These writers come up with the witty, wise, or cryptic fortunes found inside fortune cookies.

- ☐ Pet Food Taster: Pet food tasters sample pet food to check its nutritional value and taste quality – though they don't swallow it!

- ☐ Professional Line Stander: In places like Washington, D.C., people are paid to stand in line for others, especially for events or congressional hearings where early attendance is crucial.

- ☐ Snake Milker: Snake milkers extract venom from snakes for use in medical research and the production of antivenom.

- ☐ Foley Artist: Foley artists in the film industry create and record everyday sound effects, like footsteps or rustling leaves, to enhance the audio quality of movies.

☐ Odor Judge: These judges smell products like toothpaste and deodorant, as well as people's breath, armpits, and feet, to test the effectiveness of hygiene products.

☐ Waterslide Tester: This job requires individuals to travel to different waterparks to ensure the safety and fun of each slide.

☐ Chief Listening Officer: In some companies, a Chief Listening Officer listens to conversations about the company on social media and the internet, helping to improve customer engagement and brand image.

Cognitive Quirks

☐ Brain Power in Sleep: Even when you're sleeping, your brain is active. It's busy organizing memories, solving problems you encountered during the day, and even dreaming.

☐ Unlimited Memory Capacity: The human brain's memory capacity is considered virtually unlimited. It doesn't get "full" like a hard drive; instead, it keeps reorganizing and rebuilding itself.

☐ Decisions and Coin Flips: Sometimes when you're undecided, flipping a coin can actually help. Not for the result, but because while the coin is in the air, you suddenly know what you're hoping for.

☐ Yawning and Brain Cooling: Yawning might help cool your brain. Taking in a big breath of air can help to cool the blood going to your brain.

☐ Imaginary Friends: Many children have imaginary friends. This is a sign of a creative and social mind, helping them to develop social skills.

☐ Laughter and the Brain: Laughter isn't just a response to humor; it's a way for the brain to bond with others and diffuse tension.

☐ Dreams and Creativity: Dreams might seem strange, but they can actually be a sign of creativity. The brain tries out new ideas in dreams that wouldn't make sense when you're awake.

☐ Brain's Reaction to Sugar: Eating sugar can give you a rush of dopamine, the brain's "feel-good" neurotransmitter, which is why sweets can lift your mood.

☐ The Brain's Deceptive Tricks: Sometimes your brain can trick you into seeing things that aren't there, like patterns in random images – it's always trying to make sense of the world.

☐ Overthinking and Creativity: People who overthink might be more creative, as their brains are constantly buzzing with new ideas and possibilities.

☐ The Brain's Love for Music: Music activates many different areas of the brain, which is why it can make us feel so many emotions.

☐ Speaking to Yourself: Talking to yourself can actually be a sign of high cognitive functioning. It helps organize your thoughts and plan actions.

☐ Tickling Yourself: You can't tickle yourself because your brain anticipates the sensation, and this cancels out the response that normally makes tickling feel ticklish.

☐ The Brain's Favorite Color: The brain has a positive reaction to the color blue. It's often associated with calmness and can increase productivity.

☐ Forgetting to Make Room: Forgetting small details can actually be a sign of a healthy brain, as it clears out unimportant details to make room for new, more important information.

☐ Emotions and Decision Making: Emotions play a crucial role in decision-making. Without them, it's hard to make choices about what we want or don't want.

☐ Brain's Preference for Stories: The human brain loves stories. Narratives help us remember facts better than lists of information.

☐ Learning in Your Sleep: While sleeping, your brain can strengthen new memories, and there's evidence that you can learn new information while you sleep.

☐ The Brain's Autopilot Mode: A lot of your daily activities, like walking or eating, are done in 'autopilot mode' by your brain, which allows you to perform tasks without thinking about them too much.

☐ Brainwaves of Surfers: Surfers' brainwaves sync up with the waves of the ocean, leading to a calm and meditative state of mind.

Mind Games

☐ The Invisible Gorilla Test: In a famous experiment, people watching a video of a basketball game often miss seeing a person in a gorilla suit walk through the scene, showing how our focused attention can make us miss significant details.

☐ Rubber Hand Illusion: This illusion tricks the mind into feeling a fake rubber hand is part of one's body. When the real and fake hands are stroked simultaneously, the brain gets confused and starts to think the rubber hand is actually real.

- [ ] The McGurk Effect: This auditory illusion happens when what we see overrides what we hear. For example, if we see someone mouthing "ba" but hear "ga," we'll think they're saying "ba."

- [ ] The Stroop Effect: Try saying the color of a word's text when the word itself is a different color. For example, the word "blue" written in red ink. It's hard because your brain reads the word faster than it recognizes the color.

- [ ] The Müller-Lyer Illusion: In this visual trick, two lines of the same length appear different sizes because of the arrows at their ends. It shows how our brains judge distance and size.

- [ ] False Memories: Our memories aren't perfect recordings. Sometimes, we remember things that never happened or recall them differently from how they actually occurred.

- [ ] The Checker Shadow Illusion: This illusion proves that our brain perceives color and brightness relative to surrounding colors. In it, two squares in a shadow appear different in color but are actually the same.

- [ ] The Ames Room Illusion: In an Ames room, people or objects can appear to grow or shrink when moving across the room due to its unique, trapezoidal shape.

- [ ] The Phantom Limb Sensation: People who have lost a limb sometimes feel as if it's still there. This is because the brain's map of the body doesn't adjust to the change.

- [ ] The Tetris Effect: If you play a game like Tetris for a long time, you might start to see the shapes everywhere, even in your dreams. It's because your brain keeps processing the game even when you're not playing.

- [ ] The Autokinetic Effect: In a dark room with a small light, the light appears to move, even though it's still. This happens because, in the dark, the brain lacks visual references to stabilize the light's position.

- [ ] The Pareidolia Phenomenon: Ever seen a face in a cloud or a car's headlights? That's pareidolia, where the brain interprets random images or sounds as familiar patterns, like faces.

- [ ] The Capgras Delusion: A rare condition where people believe that a loved one has been replaced by an identical imposter. It's a strange mix-up between recognition and emotional response in the brain.

- [ ] The Placebo Effect: If you believe you're taking medicine, even if it's just a sugar pill (placebo), you can feel better. It shows how powerful our expectations can be in influencing how we feel.

- [ ] The Doorway Effect: Ever walked into a room and forgot why you're there? This is the doorway effect. Passing through a doorway signals the brain to file away your last thoughts and start a new scene.

- [ ] The Pinocchio Illusion: If you stimulate a muscle in your wrist while touching your nose, it can make you feel like your nose is growing, similar to the story of Pinocchio.

- [ ] The Bystander Effect: The more people who witness an emergency, the less likely anyone is to help. Everyone thinks someone else will take action.

☐ Change Blindness: This happens when a change in a visual stimulus goes unnoticed by the observer. For example, not noticing when a friend gets a haircut.

☐ The Ebbinghaus Illusion: Two circles of the same size look different when surrounded by larger or smaller circles. This shows how our perception of size is influenced by context.

☐ The Frequency Illusion: Once you notice something for the first time, like a new word, you start seeing it everywhere. It's not actually more frequent; you're just more aware of it.

Social Psychology

☐ The Power of Social Proof: People are more likely to do something if they see others doing it. This is called social proof, like when you choose to eat at a crowded restaurant over an empty one.

☐ Conformity and the Asch Experiment: Solomon Asch's experiment showed that people often conform to the majority opinion, even if it's obviously wrong, just to fit in with the group.

☐ The Bystander Effect: The more people present in an emergency, the less likely someone is to help. This is known as the bystander effect, where everyone assumes someone else will take action.

☐ The Halo Effect: This is when our overall impression of a person influences how we feel and think about their character. Like thinking someone is generally good because they are attractive.

☐ The Stanford Prison Experiment: This famous experiment had volunteers assigned as prisoners or guards in a mock prison. The experiment had to be stopped early because participants took their roles too seriously.

☐ The Power of a Uniform: Wearing a uniform can make people behave differently. For example, children in school uniforms might behave more formally than when wearing casual clothes.

☐ Groupthink and Decision Making: In a group, people often strive for consensus without critically testing, analyzing, and evaluating ideas, leading to poor decision-making.

☐ The Foot-in-the-Door Technique: This is when someone agrees to a small request first, making them more likely to agree to a larger request later.

☐ Milgram's Obedience Experiment: Stanley Milgram's experiment found that people are likely to follow orders given by an authority figure, even to the extent of harming others, underlining the powerful influence of authority.

☐ Cognitive Dissonance: When our actions don't align with our beliefs, it creates discomfort called cognitive dissonance. Like when someone knows smoking is bad for health but smokes anyway.

☐ The Spotlight Effect: This is the belief that everyone notices our appearance and behavior more than they actually do. It's like thinking everyone notices a small stain on your shirt.

☐ Mimicry and Social Bonding: People often mimic each other's body language, speech patterns, and emotions, which can lead to stronger social bonds and empathy.

☐ The Cheerleader Effect: People appear more attractive in a group than in isolation. This is known as the cheerleader effect.

☐ The False Consensus Effect: We often overestimate how much other people share our beliefs, attitudes, and behaviors.

☐ The Door-in-the-Face Technique: Refusing a large request first makes a person more likely to agree to a smaller request later.

☐ Social Loafing: People may put less effort into a task when they are part of a group, relying on others to pick up the slack.

☐ Deindividuation: In large groups, people can lose their sense of individual identity and can act in ways they normally wouldn't, like in mob situations.

☐ The Fundamental Attribution Error: We tend to attribute other people's actions to their personality or character, while attributing our own actions to our circumstances.

☐ The Anchoring Effect: The first piece of information we receive (like a price or an opinion) tends to heavily influence our decision-making and judgment thereafter.

☐ The Rosenthal Effect: Higher expectations lead to an increase in performance. This is also known as the Pygmalion effect, where believing in someone's potential makes them more likely to succeed.

Psychology of Lies

- [ ] Pinocchio Effect: Contrary to the story of Pinocchio, lying doesn't make your nose grow, but it can cause a slight itch or tingle due to increased blood flow.

- [ ] Frequent Liars: Studies show that most people lie several times a day, often without even realizing it. These are usually small, harmless lies, like saying you're fine when you're not.

- [ ] Lie Detector Tests: Polygraph tests, commonly known as lie detectors, don't actually detect lies. Instead, they measure physiological responses like heart rate, which can be affected by anxiety, nervousness, or even excitement.

- [ ] The Deception Expertise: Some people, such as spies, are trained to lie convincingly, often undergoing extensive training to control their physiological responses.

- [ ] Children and Lying: Children begin to lie from as young as two years old, usually to avoid punishment. As they grow, their lying abilities become more sophisticated.

- [ ] Spotting a Lie: Spotting a lie is challenging. Contrary to popular belief, avoiding eye contact or fidgeting doesn't necessarily indicate that someone is lying.

- [ ] The Truth Bias: People generally have a 'truth bias,' meaning they are naturally inclined to believe others, which makes deception easier.

- [ ] Lying and the Brain: Lying takes up more brain power than telling the truth, as it requires creating a story, maintaining consistency, and suppressing the truth.

- ☐ Pathological Liars: For some individuals, lying can be compulsive or pathological. Such people lie frequently and without apparent reason or benefit.

- ☐ White Lies: White lies are minor lies which are often considered harmless or even beneficial in maintaining social harmony.

- ☐ Cultural Differences in Lying: Attitudes towards lying vary across cultures. In some societies, certain types of lying are seen as a necessary part of polite interaction.

- ☐ Microexpressions: Microexpressions are brief, involuntary facial expressions that can reveal true emotions, potentially indicating if someone is lying.

- ☐ Lies in Written vs. Spoken Language: Lies in written language tend to be shorter and less detailed than truthful accounts, whereas spoken lies might involve more details to make them believable.

- ☐ The Illusion of Transparency: Liars often overestimate how easily others can see through their lies, a phenomenon known as the illusion of transparency.

- ☐ Memory and Lying: Lying can affect memory. Creating a false story can create confusion and interfere with the liar's ability to remember real events.

- ☐ Psychological Cost of Lying: Habitual lying can lead to psychological stress, guilt, and anxiety, especially if the lie is significant or ongoing.

- ☐ Lying for Survival: In some situations, lying is a survival mechanism, used to protect oneself from danger or harm.

☐ Detecting Lies in Others: Some people are better at detecting lies than others, but even the best aren't much better than chance.

☐ Body Language Myths: Common beliefs, like liars touch their nose or cover their mouth, are largely myths and not reliable indicators of deception.

☐ The Othello Error: Sometimes, the anxiety of being falsely accused can make an innocent person appear guilty, known as the Othello error.

Memory and Memories

☐ Memory and Smell: The sense of smell is closely linked to memory. A familiar scent can trigger memories more vividly than other cues.

☐ Sleep and Memory: Sleep plays a crucial role in memory consolidation. When you sleep, your brain organizes and stores your memories from the day.

☐ The First Memory Age: Most people can't remember anything from before they were about 3 or 4 years old, a phenomenon known as childhood amnesia.

☐ Déjà Vu: Déjà vu, the feeling that you've experienced something before, happens to about two-thirds of people and is thought to be a glitch in memory recall.

☐ Memory Champions: There are memory championships where competitors memorize hundreds of names, numbers, and other data. They often use techniques like the 'memory palace' to recall vast amounts of information.

- [ ] The Mandela Effect: This is when a large group of people remembers something differently than how it occurred. It's named after Nelson Mandela, whom many people falsely remembered as dying in prison in the 1980s.

- [ ] Photographic Memory: Photographic memory, the ability to recall pages of text or numbers in great detail, is extremely rare. Most people who have good memories use mnemonic devices.

- [ ] False Memories: It's possible to have memories of events that never happened. This can occur through suggestion or misinterpreting dreams as real memories.

- [ ] Memory Improvement with Age: While short-term memory may decline with age, other types of memory, like semantic memory (knowledge of facts), can improve.

- [ ] Animals and Memory: Many animals have impressive memories. For instance, crows can remember human faces associated with stressful events for years.

- [ ] Memory and Emotions: Emotional events are often remembered more vividly. This is because the brain's amygdala is activated during emotional events, strengthening the memory.

- [ ] Super Recognizers: Some people, known as super recognizers, can remember and recognize almost every face they have ever seen.

- [ ] Muscle Memory: Muscle memory isn't actually stored in your muscles; it's a type of procedural memory that helps you perform certain tasks without conscious effort, like riding a bike.

- ☐ Memory and Colors: Studies suggest that memory recall is better for colored images than black and white ones.

- ☐ The Forgetting Curve: Hermann Ebbinghaus' forgetting curve shows that memory retention declines rapidly over time unless the information is consciously reviewed.

- ☐ Tip of the Tongue Phenomenon: When you can't quite recall a word but feel it's just on the tip of your tongue, it's an actual psychological phenomenon called "lethologica."

- ☐ Memory and Boredom: Being bored can make you more creative because a bored mind searches for stimulation, which can trigger new ideas and memories.

- ☐ Flashbulb Memories: These are vivid, detailed memories of significant events. For instance, many people remember exactly where they were and what they were doing during major historical events.

- ☐ Memory and Music: Music can trigger memories and emotions. That's why songs from the past can make you nostalgic.

Color Psychology

- ☐ Blue for Creativity: Blue is often associated with creativity and calmness. Seeing the color blue can stimulate creative thinking and help with relaxation.

- ☐ Red Increases Heart Rate: Red can actually increase your heart rate and create a sense of urgency. That's why it's often used in sale signs.

☐ Yellow's Effect on Babies: Interestingly, babies tend to cry more in yellow rooms. This color is bright and attention-grabbing, but it can also be overwhelming for little ones.

☐ Green for Concentration: Green is considered one of the most restful colors for the eyes and can improve efficiency and focus.

☐ Color Blindness: Color blindness doesn't usually mean seeing in black and white. Most color-blind people can see colors, but they have difficulty distinguishing between certain shades.

☐ Orange and Appetite: Orange is known to stimulate appetite and is a common color in restaurants. It's also associated with affordability.

☐ Pink for Calmness: Pink has a calming effect and is sometimes used in prisons to calm inmates. However, over time, the effect can wear off.

☐ Black's Authority: Black is often seen as a color of authority and power. It's also associated with sophistication, which is why it's popular in fashion.

☐ White's Cleanliness: White is associated with purity and cleanliness, which is why doctors and nurses often wear white.

☐ Purple's Royal Connection: Historically, purple dye was rare and expensive, so it's associated with luxury, wealth, and royalty.

☐ Warm vs. Cool Colors: Warm colors, like red and yellow, are stimulating, while cool colors, like blue and green, are calming.

- ☐ Synesthesia: Some people experience synesthesia, where they perceive colors when they see certain numbers or hear sounds, effectively blending their senses.

- ☐ The Isolation Effect: Known as the von Restorff effect, items that stand out (like a red apple among green apples) are more likely to be remembered.

- ☐ Gender Differences in Color Perception: Studies suggest that women and men might perceive colors differently. Women often have a finer distinction for colors in the red spectrum.

- ☐ The Color of Night Vision: Our night vision is mostly in black and white because the rods in our eyes, which work better in low light, don't detect color.

- ☐ Cultural Differences in Color: Colors have different meanings in different cultures. For example, white is often a color of mourning in Eastern cultures, while it represents purity in Western cultures.

- ☐ Sports Teams and Red: Teams wearing red uniforms are more likely to win in sports. The color red is associated with dominance and aggression.

- ☐ 'The Dress' Phenomenon: In 2015, a photo of a dress divided the internet because people couldn't agree on its color - some saw blue and black, while others saw white and gold, highlighting differences in color perception.

- ☐ Traffic Lights and Colorblindness: People with red-green color blindness can still differentiate traffic lights by their position and brightness.

- ☐ Influence of Lighting on Color: The color of light affects how we perceive the color of objects. For example, under a blue sky, things can appear bluer.

Social Norms

- [ ] **Yawning is Contagious:** When one person yawns, it often triggers others to do the same. This is a social norm known as contagious yawning, which might be linked to empathy and group bonding.

- [ ] **Elevator Etiquette:** In most cultures, it's an unwritten social norm to face the door while riding in an elevator. People tend to automatically turn their backs to others, creating personal space.

- [ ] **Laugh Tracks on TV:** Laugh tracks are often used in TV shows to cue viewers that something is funny, encouraging laughter even if the joke isn't that great.

- [ ] **Fashion Trends:** Fashion norms change rapidly. What's trendy one year can be outdated the next. These norms are often set by celebrities and designers and followed by the public.

- [ ] **Social Media Likes:** In the digital age, getting 'likes' on social media has become a social norm, often influencing people's feelings of self-worth or popularity.

- [ ] **Driving on a Particular Side:** The norm of driving on the right or left side of the road varies by country and is strictly adhered to for safety, showing how norms can be crucial in certain contexts.

- [ ] **Personal Space Varies by Culture:** In some cultures, standing close to someone is normal, while in others, it's seen as invasive. This social norm varies greatly around the world.

- [ ] **Silence in Libraries:** The norm of being quiet in libraries isn't just about being respectful; it's rooted in the history of libraries as places for solitary study.

- [ ] Birthday Celebrations: The way people celebrate birthdays, including singing "Happy Birthday," blowing out candles, and making a wish, are social norms that vary but are widely accepted across cultures.

- [ ] Queueing: In many cultures, standing in line or queueing is a strong social norm. Cutting in line is generally frowned upon and can cause public disapproval.

- [ ] The Norm of Reciprocity: If someone does something for you, there's a social norm that you should do something in return. This norm is a fundamental part of human interactions.

- [ ] Table Manners: Social norms dictate good table manners, like not talking with your mouth full or using utensils properly, varying significantly across cultures.

- [ ] Tipping in Restaurants: In some countries, tipping is a social norm and even mandatory, while in others, it's not expected or can even be considered rude.

- [ ] Saying "Bless You": Saying "bless you" when someone sneezes is a norm in many cultures, originally believed to ward off evil spirits or as a wish for good health.

- [ ] Holiday Traditions: From decorating Christmas trees to lighting Hanukkah candles, holiday traditions are social norms that vary by culture but are deeply ingrained and widely practiced.

- [ ] Shaking Hands: Shaking hands is a common greeting in many cultures, but it's not universal. In some places, bowing or kissing on the cheek is the norm.

- [ ] Fashion Faux Pas: Wearing socks with sandals is often considered a fashion faux pas, showing how social norms also dictate what is considered a fashion mistake.

- [ ] Superstitions: Many social norms are based on superstitions, like avoiding walking under ladders or knocking on wood for good luck.

- [ ] Public Speaking Etiquette: It's a norm to be quiet and attentive when someone is speaking in public settings, such as during a lecture or presentation.

- [ ] Eating Times: The norm for meal times varies by culture. For instance, dinner is eaten earlier in some countries and later in others, often depending on work schedules and lifestyle.

Social Networks

- [ ] The First Social Media Site: Believe it or not, the first social media site was called "Six Degrees," created in 1997, long before Facebook and Twitter.

- [ ] Facebook's User Base: If Facebook were a country, it would be the largest in the world based on population, surpassing China and India.

- [ ] The Power of Hashtags: Hashtags started on Twitter, and now they're used everywhere to connect conversations and topics across the globe.

- [ ] Instagram's First Photo: The first photo ever posted on Instagram was of a dog near a taco stand, taken by one of Instagram's co-founders.

☐ Retweets vs. Original Tweets: Studies have found that lies spread faster than the truth on Twitter, especially when it comes to retweets.

☐ Emoji Language: Emojis have become a universal language on social media, transcending language barriers and allowing people to express emotions easily.

☐ Snapchat's Self-Destructing Messages: Snapchat revolutionized social media with messages that disappear after being viewed, promoting a more spontaneous way of sharing.

☐ LinkedIn's Professional Network: LinkedIn is the largest professional network on the internet, with members from almost every country in the world.

☐ YouTube's Massive Viewership: Every minute, more than 500 hours of video are uploaded to YouTube, offering a vast array of content from educational to entertainment.

☐ The Ice Bucket Challenge: One of the most viral social media campaigns was the ALS Ice Bucket Challenge, raising awareness and funds for amyotrophic lateral sclerosis research.

☐ Twitter's Original Character Limit: Twitter initially limited posts to 140 characters, based on the character limit of a standard text message.

☐ Facebook's Blue Color Scheme: Facebook is blue because its creator, Mark Zuckerberg, has red-green color blindness, and blue is the richest color for him.

☐ TikTok's Rise: TikTok became one of the fastest-growing social media platforms, known for its short, catchy videos and wide appeal among younger audiences.

- ☐ Pinterest as a Planning Tool: Pinterest is often used for planning important life events, like weddings or home renovations, serving as a digital inspiration board.

- ☐ Virtual Flash Mobs: Social media has enabled the coordination of virtual flash mobs, where people gather suddenly in public places to perform or protest, organized entirely online.

- ☐ The Birth of Social Media Influencers: Social media has created a new career path - the influencer, who can impact trends and market products to their followers.

- ☐ Facebook's 'Like' Button: The 'Like' button on Facebook was almost called the 'Awesome' button. It's now a universal symbol for showing approval on social media.

- ☐ Myspace's Influence: Myspace, one of the first social networks, was instrumental in launching the careers of several musicians and artists, showcasing the power of social media in the entertainment industry.

- ☐ WhatsApp's Global Reach: WhatsApp is hugely popular for messaging, especially in countries outside the USA, due to its ease of use and ability to send messages over the internet.

- ☐ Social Media and Pets: Pets often have their own social media profiles, managed by their owners, with some pets becoming famous and even earning money through endorsements and appearances.

Verbal Blunders

- ☐ "Excuse My French": Sometimes when people make a language error or curse, they say "excuse my French," a humorous way to apologize for their slip-up, even though what they said wasn't actually French.

- [ ] Spoonerisms: Named after Reverend William Archibald Spooner, spoonerisms occur when the initial sounds of words are swapped by mistake, like saying "a well-boiled icicle" instead of "a well-oiled bicycle."

- [ ] Freudian Slips: Named after Sigmund Freud, these are slip-ups in speech that supposedly reveal something about your subconscious thoughts, like accidentally calling your teacher "Mom."

- [ ] Bushisms: Former U.S. President George W. Bush was known for his language gaffes, called "Bushisms," like saying "They misunderestimated me."

- [ ] Yogi Berra's Malapropisms: Famous baseball player Yogi Berra was known for his humorous language mistakes called malapropisms, like saying "Texas has a lot of electrical votes" instead of "electoral votes."

- [ ] "All Intensive Purposes": A common misphrase is "all intensive purposes," which is actually "all intents and purposes."

- [ ] "For All In Tents and Campfires": A playful twist on the previous phrase, this humorous misinterpretation imagines a scenario involving tents and campfires.

- [ ] Eggcorns: An eggcorn is a word or phrase that sounds similar to and is mistakenly used in a seemingly logical or plausible way for the correct word, like saying "old-timer's disease" instead of "Alzheimer's disease."

- [ ] "I Could Care Less": Often used to mean "I couldn't care less," this common mistake actually implies that you do care, at least a little.

☐ Mondegreens: Misheard lyrics in songs are called mondegreens. A famous example is hearing "'Scuse me while I kiss this guy" instead of Jimi Hendrix's actual lyric, "'Scuse me while I kiss the sky."

☐ "Irregardless" Confusion: "Irregardless" is often used as if it means without regard, but it's a non-standard word – the correct term is "regardless."

☐ "I Literally Died": People often use "literally" for emphasis when they actually mean "figuratively," like saying, "I literally died laughing."

☐ Tongue Twisters: Tongue twisters are phrases designed to be difficult to articulate properly, and often lead to amusing mistakes, like "She sells seashells by the seashore."

☐ "Pacifically Speaking": A funny mistake is saying "pacifically" instead of "specifically." It turns a statement about details into a comment about the Pacific Ocean!

☐ "A Damp Squib": Often mistakenly said as "a damp squid," the correct phrase "a damp squib" refers to a situation that fails to meet expectations, much like a wet firework (squib) would.

☐ Autocorrect Fails: Autocorrect on phones and computers can create hilarious language errors, like changing "Let's eat, Grandma!" to "Let's eat Grandma!", which completely alters the meaning.

☐ "The World is Your Lobster": A mix-up of "The world is your oyster," this funny error swaps the mollusk for a crustacean, creating a nonsensical but humorous phrase.

☐ Double Negatives: Using two negatives can unintentionally turn the sentence into a positive, like saying "I didn't see nothing," which technically means you saw something.

☐ Mixing Metaphors: Combining two metaphors can result in a funny language mistake, like "It's not rocket surgery," mixing "rocket science" and "brain surgery."

☐ "Nip It in the Butt": The correct phrase is "nip it in the bud," referring to stopping something early on. The mistaken version gives a comically different mental image.

Global Linguistic Gems

☐ Schadenfreude (German): This word describes the feeling of joy or pleasure when one sees another person fail or suffer misfortune.

☐ Sobremesa (Spanish): The time spent after lunch or dinner, talking to the people you shared the meal with. It's a time for chatting and enjoying each other's company.

☐ Hygge (Danish): A quality of coziness that creates a feeling of contentment or well-being. It's enjoying life's simple pleasures.

☐ Tartle (Scottish): That awkward moment when you hesitate while introducing someone because you've forgotten their name.

☐ Tsundoku (Japanese): The act of acquiring books and not reading them, letting them pile up on shelves or floors.

☐ Gigil (Filipino): The irresistible urge to squeeze or pinch something that is unbearably cute, like a chubby baby's cheek.

- ☐ Komorebi (Japanese): The scattered light that filters through when sunlight shines through tree leaves.

- ☐ Iktsuarpok (Inuit): The feeling of anticipation when waiting for someone, causing you to keep going outside to check if they have arrived.

- ☐ Bakku-shan (Japanese): The experience of seeing a woman who appears pretty from behind but not from the front.

- ☐ Wabi-Sabi (Japanese): Finding beauty in imperfections, an acceptance of the cycle of life and death.

- ☐ Mångata (Swedish): The road-like reflection of the moon on the water.

- ☐ Saudade (Portuguese): A deep emotional state of nostalgic longing for someone or something that is absent.

- ☐ Utepils (Norwegian): To sit outside on a sunny day enjoying a beer.

- ☐ Kalsarikännit (Finnish): The feeling when you are going to get drunk home alone in your underwear, with no intention of going out.

- ☐ L'appel du vide (French): "The call of the void" – the instinctive urge to jump from high places.

- ☐ Gezelligheid (Dutch): The comfort and coziness of being at home, with friends or loved ones, or general togetherness.

- ☐ Fernweh (German): Feeling homesick for a place you have never been to.

- [ ] Waldeinsamkeit (German): The feeling of being alone in the woods, an interconnectedness with nature.

- [ ] Pana Po'o (Hawaiian): The act of scratching your head in order to help you remember something you've forgotten.

- [ ] Tingo (Pascuense): The act of taking objects one desires from the house of a friend by gradually borrowing all of them.

Linguistic Games

- [ ] Pig Latin: A playful language game where you take the first consonant of a word, move it to the end, and add "ay." For example, "hello" becomes "ellohay."

- [ ] Caesar Cipher: Used by Julius Caesar, it shifts each letter in a message a certain number of places down the alphabet. For instance, with a shift of 1, 'A' becomes 'B'.

- [ ] Palindrome: A word, phrase, or sequence that reads the same backward as forward. "Racecar" and "madam" are classic examples.

- [ ] Leet Speak: Originally used by hackers, it replaces letters with similar looking numbers or symbols, like using "3" for "E" or "7" for "T."

- [ ] Morse Code: A system of dots and dashes representing letters and numbers, used for telegraph messages. For example, SOS, the distress signal, is ··· — ···.

- [ ] Hieroglyphics: Ancient Egyptians used these pictorial symbols to write. Each symbol could represent a sound, an object, or an idea.

- ☐ Braille: A tactile writing system used by people who are visually impaired, Braille consists of raised dots that can be felt with the fingertips.

- ☐ Enigma Machine: Used by Germans in WWII, the Enigma machine was a complex cipher machine that encrypted messages, later famously decrypted by Allied codebreakers.

- ☐ Anagrams: Rearranging the letters of a word or phrase to create a new word or phrase, using all the original letters exactly once. For example, "listen" becomes "silent."

- ☐ Rot13: A simple letter substitution cipher that replaces a letter with the 13th letter after it in the alphabet. It's often used online to hide spoilers or puzzle solutions.

- ☐ Klingon Language: Invented for the "Star Trek" series, Klingon has its own grammar, vocabulary, and even dialects, created by linguist Marc Okrand.

- ☐ Backslang: A type of slang where words are spoken or written backward, often used to obscure the meaning from outsiders.

- ☐ Navajo Code Talkers: During World War II, the U.S. military used the Navajo language as an unbreakable code for transmitting secret tactical messages.

- ☐ Pigpen Cipher: A geometric simple substitution cipher, which uses a set of grids and dots to represent each letter.

- ☐ Ambigrams: Words or designs that retain meaning or form when viewed from different directions or perspectives.

- [ ] Spoonerisms: Accidentally swapping the first sounds of two words in a phrase, often resulting in humorous outcomes, named after Reverend W. A. Spooner.

- [ ] Talking in Opposites: A playful language game where you say the opposite of what you mean, requiring the listener to mentally translate for the actual meaning.

- [ ] Ubbi Dubbi: Popularized by the TV show "Zoom," it adds "ub" before each vowel sound in a word. For example, "hello" becomes "hubellubo."

- [ ] Vigenère Cipher: A method of encrypting text by using a series of different Caesar ciphers based on the letters of a keyword, it was considered unbreakable for centuries.

- [ ] Binary Code: Used in computers, it represents text using two symbols, typically '0' and '1'. Each letter or character is assigned a unique binary string.

Obsolete Vocabulary

- [ ] Fudgel: An 18th-century term meaning "pretending to work when you're not actually doing anything at all." Almost like modern-day slacking!

- [ ] Twattle: To gossip or chat idly about trivial matters. This word from the 17th century described what we now call small talk.

- [ ] Groak: To silently watch someone while they are eating, hoping they'll offer you some of their food.

☐ Curglaff: The shock felt when first plunging into cold water. A Scottish word that perfectly describes that freezing swim feeling!

☐ Snoutfair: A word from the 1500s that meant "a person with a handsome countenance." It's an old-fashioned way of saying someone is good-looking.

☐ Jargogle: This 17th-century word means to confuse or jumble. Nowadays, we might just say something's "muddled up."

☐ Kench: To laugh loudly. Imagine your friends "kenching" at a hilarious joke during lunch.

☐ Twitter-light: Not related to the social media platform, this charming old word describes the time of day just before dawn.

☐ Lethophobia: The fear of oblivion, used in the 1700s. It's not just about fear of death, but fear of being forgotten.

☐ Gorgonize: To have a mesmerizing effect on someone, much like the mythical Gorgon could turn people to stone with a look.

☐ Ultracrepidarian: A person who gives opinions on subjects they know nothing about. Definitely still relevant today but sadly underused!

☐ Quockerwodger: A 19th-century term for a wooden puppet. It's also used to describe a politician whose strings are pulled by someone else.

☐ Philogrobilized: Feeling hungover or unwell, but without having drunk any alcohol. It's like feeling groggy after staying up too late.

- [ ] Zwodder: A drowsy, muddled state of mind. When you wake up feeling all fuzzy and not quite there yet.

- [ ] Yex: An old word for hiccup. Imagine saying "I've got the yexes" instead of "I have hiccups."

- [ ] Lanspresado: The person who conveniently shows up after everything has been paid for, especially in a pub setting. Still a relevant concept today!

- [ ] Brabble: To argue loudly about something trivial. A brabble sounds like a noisy squabble over who ate the last cookie.

- [ ] Apricity: The warmth of the sun in winter. It's a beautiful concept that deserves more recognition.

- [ ] Fuzzle: To make drunk, slightly tipsy. Not quite a full-on drunken state, but just a bit fuzzy from a drink.

- [ ] Cockalorum: A little man with a high opinion of himself. It's an amusing and descriptive term for someone who's overly confident.

Invented Languages

- [ ] Klingon from Star Trek: Klingon, created for the "Star Trek" series, has its own grammar and vocabulary. It's so well-developed that people have translated Shakespeare's works into Klingon.

- [ ] Dothraki and Valyrian for Game of Thrones: Linguist David J. Peterson developed Dothraki and High Valyrian languages for "Game of Thrones," complete with their own unique grammar rules and vocabulary.

☐ Elvish Languages in The Lord of the Rings: J.R.R. Tolkien, a philologist, created several Elvish languages for his Middle-earth universe, including Quenya and Sindarin, with their own scripts.

☐ Na'vi for Avatar: The Na'vi language, created by linguist Paul Frommer for James Cameron's "Avatar," has over a thousand words and a complex grammatical structure.

☐ Parseltongue in Harry Potter: Parseltongue, the language of snakes in the "Harry Potter" series, sounds like hissing to most characters but is fully understood by those who speak it.

☐ Newspeak in 1984: George Orwell's novel "1984" featured Newspeak, a language designed to limit freedom of thought and control the populace.

☐ Minionese in Despicable Me: Minionese, spoken by the Minions in "Despicable Me," is a mix of many languages, including Spanish, English, and Italian, with a lot of nonsensical words and sounds.

☐ Kryptonian in Superman Comics: Kryptonian, the language of Superman's home planet, has its own alphabet and has been developed over the years in comics and movies.

☐ Simlish in The Sims: Simlish is a fictional language used in "The Sims" video game series. It's a gibberish speech that emulates the sound and cadence of real language.

☐ Thhtmaa in Arrival: For the film "Arrival," a new language called Thhtmaa was created for the alien species, with a unique circular script representing their non-linear perception of time.

- ☐ Huttese in Star Wars: Huttese, spoken by Jabba the Hutt in "Star Wars," is a mix of different languages, including Quechua, a language spoken in the Andes.

- ☐ Atlantean for Atlantis: The Lost Empire: Created by linguist Marc Okrand, the Atlantean language was designed for the Disney film "Atlantis: The Lost Empire" and was based on Indo-European roots.

- ☐ Fremen Language in Dune: In "Dune" by Frank Herbert, the Fremen language reflects their desert culture and includes words borrowed from Arabic and other real-world languages.

- ☐ Tengwar Script in The Lord of the Rings: The Tengwar script, used for writing Elvish and other languages in Tolkien's world, has a beautiful, flowing script that fans often use for artistic purposes.

- ☐ Vulcan Language in Star Trek: Alongside Klingon, the Vulcan language was also developed for "Star Trek," featuring its own unique script and phrases.

- ☐ Groot's Language in Guardians of the Galaxy: Groot from "Guardians of the Galaxy" only says "I am Groot," but it's implied that these few words have a multitude of meanings, understood by his companion Rocket.

- ☐ Ferengi Language in Star Trek: The Ferengi language, another creation for "Star Trek," reflects the commerce-oriented culture of the Ferengi people.

- ☐ The Ancient Language in Eragon: In the "Eragon" series by Christopher Paolini, the Ancient Language is used to cast spells and has its own grammar and vocabulary.

- ☐ Lapine Language in Watership Down: Lapine, the language of the rabbits in Richard Adams'

"Watership Down," includes words like "tharn" (stunned and scared) and "silflay" (going aboveground to feed).

- [ ] The Universal Translator Concept: In many sci-fi universes, like "Star Trek," a fictional universal translator device helps characters understand and communicate in different alien languages instantly.

Philosophical Puzzles

- [ ] The Chicken or the Egg: Which came first? This age-old question challenges the concept of cause and effect and has puzzled philosophers and scientists alike.

- [ ] The Ship of Theseus: If you replace every part of a ship over time, is it still the same ship? This paradox explores the nature of identity and change.

- [ ] The Paradox of the Court: A man promises to pay his teacher after winning his first case. The teacher sues him for payment after he graduates, but he hasn't won a case yet. If he wins this case, he loses by his own argument.

- [ ] Zeno's Paradoxes: Ancient philosopher Zeno proposed paradoxes like the "Arrow Paradox," suggesting that motion is an illusion because an arrow in flight occupies a space equal to itself, thus seeming motionless.

- [ ] The Trolley Problem: Would you pull a lever to divert a runaway trolley onto a track where it will hit one person, to save five on another track? This thought experiment explores moral dilemmas.

- [ ] Schrödinger's Cat: A cat in a box could be alive or dead, and until the box is opened, it's considered to be both. This paradox questions the nature of reality and observation.

☐ The Barber Paradox: A barber shaves everyone who does not shave themselves. Who shaves the barber? If he shaves himself, he cannot shave himself by his own rule.

☐ The Paradox of the Stone: Can an omnipotent being create a stone so heavy that even they cannot lift it? This philosophical puzzle challenges the concept of omnipotence.

☐ The Infinite Monkey Theorem: Given infinite time, a monkey typing randomly could eventually type out the complete works of Shakespeare. This paradox explores probability and infinity.

☐ The Grandfather Paradox: If you travel back in time and accidentally prevent your grandfather from meeting your grandmother, you would never be born to travel back in time in the first place.

☐ The Paradox of Thrift: If everyone saves money during a recession, the economy will actually worsen because spending decreases, highlighting a contradiction in economic behavior.

☐ Russell's Paradox: Bertrand Russell proposed a paradox involving sets. If a set contains all sets that do not contain themselves, does it contain itself?

☐ The Twin Paradox: In Einstein's theory of relativity, if one twin travels into space at high speed and returns, they would be younger than the twin who stayed on Earth.

☐ The Unexpected Hanging: A judge tells a condemned prisoner that he will be hanged at noon on one weekday in the following week but that the execution will be a surprise. The prisoner concludes it can't happen, but it does.

☐ The Omnipotence Paradox: Can an omnipotent being create a task that it cannot accomplish? This paradox explores the limits of absolute power.

☐ The Sorites Paradox: If you remove grains from a heap of sand one by one, at what point does it stop being a heap? This paradox explores vagueness and the problem of fuzzy concepts.

☐ The Crocodile Dilemma: A crocodile snatches a child and promises to return the child if the mother correctly guesses what the crocodile will do. What happens if the mother says the crocodile will not return her child?

☐ The Paradox of Fiction: How can we feel genuine emotions about characters and events we know are fictional? This paradox explores the nature of emotional responses to art.

☐ The Paradox of Free Will and Determinism: If our actions are determined by past events, can we truly have free will? This paradox challenges the concept of free choice.

☐ The Paradox of the Liar: This paradox involves a sentence saying "This sentence is false." If it's true, then it must be false, but if it's false, it must be true.

Philosophical Humor

☐ Diogenes and the Sun: Diogenes, the Greek philosopher, once saw a young man drinking from his hands. He threw away his cup, saying, "A child has beaten me in plainness of living."

- ☐ Socrates and the Marketplace: Socrates was once found wandering in a marketplace. When asked what he was doing, he replied, "I am looking to see how many things there are which I do not want."

- ☐ Voltaire's Wit: Voltaire, known for his sharp wit, was asked on his deathbed to renounce Satan. He replied, "This is no time to be making new enemies."

- ☐ Bertrand Russell's Teapot: Russell famously said that if he claimed a teapot was orbiting the Sun between Earth and Mars, it was nonsense for others to expect him to prove it; rather, it was their job to prove him wrong.

- ☐ Karl Marx and Profit: Karl Marx reportedly said, "I am not a Marxist," humorously distancing himself from some interpretations of his own theories.

- ☐ Nietzsche and Dancing: Nietzsche once said, "And those who were seen dancing were thought to be insane by those who could not hear the music." A quote emphasizing perception and understanding.

- ☐ Confucius and the Finger: Confucius said, "When a wise man points at the moon, the imbecile examines the finger." This highlights focusing on the important things rather than the trivial.

- ☐ Aristotle and Happiness: Aristotle was asked, "What is a friend?" He replied, "A single soul dwelling in two bodies." He valued the deep connection and understanding between friends.

- ☐ Plato's Featherless Bipeds: Plato defined humans as featherless bipeds. Diogenes plucked a chicken and brought it into Plato's Academy, saying, "Here is Plato's human!"

- [ ] Descartes' Dreams: René Descartes once dreamt about a dictionary and a book of poetry. He interpreted this as the union of science and art in philosophy.

- [ ] Zeno's Paradoxes: Zeno of Elea, known for his paradoxes, reportedly raced a tortoise as a joke to illustrate his paradox of motion, in which he always gave the tortoise a head start.

- [ ] Thomas Aquinas' Size: Legend has it that Thomas Aquinas was so large, his monastery had a table with a section cut out to accommodate his belly.

- [ ] David Hume and the Mud: David Hume once got stuck in a swamp. A farmer refused to help him out until Hume admitted that practical knowledge (like farming) was more useful than philosophical knowledge.

- [ ] Jean-Paul Sartre and the Nobel Prize: When awarded the Nobel Prize in Literature, Sartre famously refused it, stating he always declined official honors.

- [ ] Laozi and Simplicity: Laozi, the ancient Chinese philosopher, said, "A journey of a thousand miles begins with a single step," emphasizing the importance of simplicity and patience.

- [ ] Immanuel Kant's Routine: Kant was so punctual and routine in his daily walks that neighbors would set their clocks by his movements.

- [ ] Wittgenstein and the Poker: During a heated philosophy debate, Ludwig Wittgenstein reportedly threatened fellow philosopher Karl Popper with a fireplace poker.

- [ ] Heraclitus and Change: Heraclitus believed that change is central to the universe, famously saying, "No man ever steps in the same river twice."

- [ ] Spinoza's Lens Grinding: Baruch Spinoza, a philosopher, made his living grinding lenses, showing his belief in combining theoretical and practical work.

- [ ] Schopenhauer and Poodles: Arthur Schopenhauer, known for his pessimism, had a succession of poodles, all named Atma, after the Sanskrit word for "world soul."

Sayings from Philosophers

- [ ] Diogenes: "I am a citizen of the world," declared Diogenes, the Greek philosopher, when asked where he came from – showing his belief in being part of a larger community than just his city-state.

- [ ] Socrates: "I know that I am intelligent, because I know that I know nothing." This witty paradox by Socrates reflects his belief in the importance of questioning and acknowledging one's own ignorance.

- [ ] Voltaire: "The more I read, the more I acquire, the more certain I am that I know nothing." A humorous take on the endless pursuit of knowledge.

- [ ] Nietzsche: "I'm not upset that you lied to me, I'm upset that from now on I can't believe you." Friedrich Nietzsche's clever way of expressing the impact of broken trust.

- [ ] Aristotle: "The worst form of inequality is to try to make unequal things equal." A witty observation on the complexity of fairness and justice.

☐ Plato: "Wise men speak because they have something to say; fools because they have to say something." Plato's humorous distinction between wisdom and foolishness.

☐ Confucius: "Man who stand on hill with mouth open will wait a long time for roast duck to drop in." A funny way to say that success comes from action, not waiting.

☐ Bertrand Russell: "The trouble with the world is that the stupid are cocksure and the intelligent are full of doubt." A humorous yet poignant observation on human nature.

☐ Karl Marx: "History repeats itself, first as tragedy, second as farce." Marx's witty take on the cyclical nature of history.

☐ Jean-Paul Sartre: "If you're lonely when you're alone, you're in bad company." A clever way of saying that you should be comfortable with yourself.

☐ Laozi: "A journey of a thousand miles begins with a single step...and a lot of complaining." A humorous twist on the famous quote, adding a bit of reality to the idea of starting a big task.

☐ Descartes: "It is not enough to have a good mind; the main thing is to use it well." Descartes' witty reminder about the importance of practical application of intelligence.

☐ Heraclitus: "No man ever steps in the same river twice, for it's not the same river and he's not the same man." A clever observation about change and continuity.

☐ Immanuel Kant: "Science is organized knowledge. Wisdom is organized life." Kant's witty distinction between knowledge and wisdom.

☐ Zeno of Elea: Famous for his paradoxes, Zeno humorously challenged the notion of motion, arguing, "Motion is nothing but an illusion!"

☐ George Santayana: "Those who cannot remember the past are condemned to repeat it – but they'll never realize it." A funny yet wise take on the importance of learning from history.

☐ Thomas Aquinas: "Beware the man of a single book." Aquinas' humorous way of warning against those who base their beliefs on only one perspective.

☐ Spinoza: "I have striven not to laugh at human actions, not to weep at them, nor to hate them, but to understand them." A witty perspective on the study of human behavior.

☐ Schopenhauer: "Life is a business that does not cover the costs." A darkly humorous take on the existential dilemma of life.

☐ David Hume: "Beauty in things exists in the mind which contemplates them." Hume's clever comment on the subjectivity of beauty and perception.

Funny Inventions

☐ Pet Rock: Invented in 1975, the Pet Rock was a smooth stone sold in a box with breathing holes and straw. It was marketed as the perfect pet, requiring no feeding or care.

☐ The Useless Box: This amusing gadget's only function is to turn itself off. When you flip the switch on, a little arm pops out and turns it back off.

☐ Spaghetti Fork: A fork with a built-in motor that twirls the spaghetti for you. It's designed for those who struggle with the art of twirling pasta on a fork.

☐ Diet Water: In Japan, diet water was introduced for those who wanted all the benefits of regular water, but with fewer calories, despite water having no calories to begin with.

☐ Banana Slicer: A plastic tool that slices a whole banana into even pieces in one go. It's oddly specific but oddly satisfying to use.

☐ Goldfish Walker: An invention for taking your goldfish on a walk, it's essentially a fishbowl on wheels, allowing your fish to see the world.

☐ USB Pet Rock: A modern twist on the original Pet Rock, this version plugs into your USB port but does absolutely nothing, just like the original.

☐ Duck-Billed Protective Muzzle for Dogs: A muzzle that makes your dog look like it has a duck bill, turning a safety device into a source of amusement.

☐ The Baby Mop: An outfit for babies with mop-like fringes on the arms and legs, so your baby cleans the floor as it crawls around.

☐ Shoe Umbrellas: Tiny umbrellas for your shoes to keep them dry in the rain. They're more comical than practical.

☐ The Selfie Toaster: A toaster that can toast your selfie onto a piece of bread. It uses custom heating inserts based on a photo you provide.

☐ Hug Me Pillow: A pillow shaped like a human torso with an arm, designed to make you feel like you're being hugged while you sleep.

☐ The Ostrich Pillow: A pillow you can put your entire head and hands into for napping anywhere. It looks like an oversized soft helmet with holes for breathing and resting your hands.

☐ The Walking Sleeping Bag: A sleeping bag with legs, so you can walk around while staying cozy. It's perfect for those who get cold easily during camping trips.

☐ Butter Stick: A glue-stick-style container filled with butter, allowing you to spread butter on toast as if you were applying glue.

☐ The TV Hat: A hat with a long bill and a drop-down screen for your smartphone, giving you a private movie theater experience.

☐ Noodle Fan: A small fan attached to chopsticks that cools down hot noodles as you lift them to your mouth.

☐ Square Watermelons: In Japan, watermelons are grown in square boxes to shape them into cubes, making them easier to stack and store.

☐ The Necktie Flask: A tie with a hidden flask inside. It's meant for those who need a discreet sip while maintaining a professional appearance.

☐ The 360-Degree Camera Hat: A hat with cameras all around it to capture a 360-degree view. It's like Google Street View on your head.

Inventions by Kids

☐ Popsicles: In 1905, 11-year-old Frank Epperson left a mixture of powdered soda, water, and a stirring stick in a cup outside overnight. It froze, and the Popsicle was born!

☐ Earmuffs: Chester Greenwood, at the age of 15, invented earmuffs in 1873 to keep his ears warm during the harsh Maine winter. He patented his idea and made a fortune.

☐ Trampolines: In 1930, 16-year-old George Nissen saw trapeze artists performing tricks when dismounting into the safety net and got inspired. He created the first trampoline in his garage.

☐ Braille: Louis Braille invented the Braille system of reading and writing for the blind at just 15 years old, transforming the way visually impaired individuals interact with the world.

☐ Christmas Lights: In 1917, 15-year-old Albert Sadacca came up with the idea of electric Christmas tree lights after a tragic fire caused by candles on a tree.

☐ Water Talkies: Richie Stachowski, at 11 years old, invented a device in 1996 that allowed people to talk underwater, known as the Water Talkie.

☐ Snowmobiles: At just 15, Joseph-Armand Bombardier built the first prototype of the snowmobile in 1922, revolutionizing winter travel in snowy regions.

- [ ] Oink-a-Saurus App: Fabian Fernandez-Han, at age 12, invented this app to help kids learn about finance and saving money in a fun and interactive way.

- [ ] Makenna's Magic Earplugs: Makenna, at the age of 8, created a unique type of earplug for her father who worked in construction, helping him sleep when he came home from night shifts.

- [ ] Super-Slippery Coating: At 14, Jayden Côté developed a super-slippery coating that helps reduce waste in containers like ketchup bottles and paint cans.

- [ ] The "Crayon Holder": Cassidy Goldstein, at 11 years old, solved a common problem by creating a crayon holder that helps to hold and use crayons even when they are too small to grip.

- [ ] Solar-Powered Water Purifier: At 14, Deepika Kurup invented a solar-powered water purification system, aiming to solve the global water crisis.

- [ ] iAid Navigation Tool: Alex Deans, at just 12 years old, created iAid, a navigation device for the visually impaired, using GPS and compass technology.

- [ ] The Wristies: At age 9, Kaylie invented Wristies, a type of fingerless glove that keeps your wrists and hands warm, after getting cold during piano lessons.

- [ ] Beckham's Jockstrap: Young Beckham Zobrist created a scented jockstrap to tackle the problem of bad odors in athletes' gear.

- [ ] The "Spooler": A device invented by Houston Gunn at age 13, the Spooler helps to easily reload fishing poles, a task that was difficult and time-consuming.

- [ ] Frogglez Goggles: Christian, at the age of 6, came up with an idea for comfortable swim goggles that won't pull hair or leak, known as Frogglez.

- [ ] Removable Stickers: At age 8, Robert Patch created a toy truck with removable and interchangeable parts using Velcro, which he patented.

- [ ] **The "Hot Seat": Alissa Chavez, as a high school student, developed the Hot Seat, an alarm system to prevent children from being left behind in hot cars.

- [ ] The "Buggyguard": A 12-year-old invented a lock for strollers, called the Buggyguard, to prevent stroller theft at places like amusement parks and malls.

World-Altering Innovations

- [ ] The Wheel: Invented over 5,000 years ago, the wheel is considered one of the most important inventions in human history, revolutionizing transportation and machinery.

- [ ] The Printing Press: Invented by Johannes Gutenberg in the 15th century, it allowed books to be mass-produced, spreading knowledge and literacy at an unprecedented rate.

- [ ] Penicillin: Discovered by Alexander Fleming in 1928, this antibiotic has saved countless lives by treating bacterial infections.

- [ ] The Internet: Initially a project named ARPANET in the 1960s, the internet has evolved into a global network connecting billions, transforming communication and information access.

- [ ] Electricity: The harnessing and use of electricity has been pivotal in the development of modern society, powering homes, industries, and technology.

- [ ] The Telephone: Invented by Alexander Graham Bell in 1876, it drastically changed how people communicate over long distances.

- [ ] The Light Bulb: Thomas Edison's 1879 invention brought artificial light to homes and streets, extending productive hours past sunset.

- [ ] Vaccines: The development of vaccines, beginning with Edward Jenner's smallpox vaccine in 1796, has been vital in preventing diseases and saving lives.

- [ ] The Automobile: Karl Benz's 1885 invention of the motor car transformed personal transportation, leading to the global network of roads and highways we have today.

- [ ] Airplanes: The Wright Brothers' first successful flight in 1903 made long-distance travel faster, shrinking the world in terms of travel time.

- [ ] Personal Computers: From the first Apple computers to today's laptops, personal computers have democratized access to technology and information.

- [ ] The Compass: Invented in ancient China, the magnetic compass was crucial for navigation at sea, allowing explorers to travel across oceans.

- [ ] The Telescope: Invented in the early 17th century, telescopes opened up the universe for exploration, significantly impacting astronomy.

- [ ] The Steam Engine: Pioneered by James Watt, the steam engine fueled the Industrial Revolution, changing the way products were manufactured and transported.

☐ The Refrigerator: This invention transformed the way food is stored and preserved, greatly impacting daily life and food safety.

☐ The Camera: The invention of the camera captured moments in time, leading to the vast and varied world of photography we know today.

☐ The Microwave Oven: Invented by Percy Spencer in 1945, the microwave oven revolutionized cooking and food preparation.

☐ Plastic: The development of synthetic plastics has had a massive impact on manufacturing, packaging, and a wide array of products.

☐ The Sewing Machine: Invented in the 19th century, the sewing machine greatly increased the efficiency of clothing production.

☐ The World Wide Web: Proposed by Tim Berners-Lee in 1989, it made the internet accessible and user-friendly, leading to the digital age we live in today.

Weirdest Patents

☐ Anti-Eating Face Mask: This odd invention patented in 1982 is designed to prevent overeating. It's a mask that locks over your mouth to make eating inconvenient.

☐ High-Five Machine: Patented in 1993, this device allows users to simulate a high-five when no one else is around. It's essentially a mechanical arm mounted on a wall.

- ☐ Animal Ear Protectors: Invented to protect animals like dogs and horses from getting water in their ears during baths or rainy weather, these ear protectors are both funny and practical.

- ☐ Flatulence Deodorizer: This patent includes a pad that can be attached to underwear, filtering out bad odors caused by flatulence.

- ☐ Portable Nuclear Shelter: Patented during the Cold War, this invention is a small, personal nuclear shelter designed to be worn as a backpack.

- ☐ Geriatric Communication Device: A system patented for the elderly to summon help, which is essentially a complex series of tubes and speaking devices, quite like an old-school intercom.

- ☐ Banana Suitcase: A travel case specifically designed for transporting a single banana. It's a hard shell case shaped like a banana to prevent bruising.

- ☐ Hiccup Treatment Device: A patented device that claims to cure hiccups. The user drinks water from a cup while pulling a string, creating gentle pressure thought to stop hiccups.

- ☐ Bird Diaper: A diaper for pet birds, allowing them to freely roam around the house without making a mess.

- ☐ Beerbrella: A small umbrella for your beer, invented to keep your drink shaded and cool on sunny days. It attaches right to the beer can or glass.

- ☐ Comb-over Haircut Patent: Believe it or not, someone patented a method for styling hair to cover bald spots, better known as the comb-over, in 1977.

- [ ] The Smoker's Hat: A hat designed with an umbrella-like structure to shelter a smoker in the rain, with a special holder for the cigarette.

- [ ] The "Wearable" Dog Washer: A ring-like device that attaches to a hose, designed to wash a dog by creating a water curtain around them.

- [ ] Life Expectancy Watch: A watch that supposedly calculates and displays the wearer's expected life span, though its accuracy is, of course, debatable.

- [ ] Dynamite Alarm Clock: A rather extreme invention intended to wake up deep sleepers. When the alarm goes off, it lights a candle which eventually explodes a small amount of dynamite.

- [ ] Goatee Saver: A grooming device that acts as a template to shave around, ensuring a perfectly shaped goatee every time.

- [ ] Spaghetti Fork: This battery-operated fork automatically winds spaghetti onto the fork, making it easier to eat without making a mess.

- [ ] The "Kissing Shield": Invented in the late 19th century, it's a device that two people wear over their mouths while kissing to prevent the spread of germs.

- [ ] Human Slingshot: This patent involves a large slingshot designed to fling a person across a distance, intended for entertainment purposes.

Timeless Innovations

- [ ] Da Vinci's Flying Machines: Leonardo da Vinci sketched designs for various flying machines in the

15th century, including a helicopter-like "aerial screw" and a hang glider, centuries before the first airplane.

- [ ] The Antikythera Mechanism: Discovered in a shipwreck from around 200 BC, this ancient Greek device is an intricate mechanism that tracked celestial bodies and eclipses, resembling an early computer.

- [ ] Jules Verne's Submarine: In his 1870 novel "Twenty Thousand Leagues Under the Sea," Jules Verne imagined a submarine powered by electricity, decades before such technology became a reality.

- [ ] The Baghdad Battery: Dating back to the Parthian period (250 BC to AD 250), these clay jars may have been used as galvanic cells for electroplating gold onto silver, long before modern batteries.

- [ ] Hero's Steam Engine: In the 1st century AD, Greek mathematician Hero of Alexandria created the first recorded steam engine, called an aeolipile, but it was never used for practical purposes.

- [ ] Automata: Ancient Greeks and Egyptians created automata, which were essentially early forms of robots, used in temples and to perform simple tasks.

- [ ] Charles Babbage's Analytical Engine: Designed in the 1830s, this was a mechanical general-purpose computer that laid the groundwork for the modern computer.

- [ ] Nikola Tesla's Wireless Power: In the late 19th century, Tesla experimented with wireless lighting and power distribution, a concept only now becoming widely explored.

- [ ] The Aeolipile: An early jet engine concept, the aeolipile was a sphere mounted so that it could turn on steam jets, invented by Hero of Alexandria around 100 BC.

- [ ] Giovanni Fontana's Robot: In the 15th century, this Italian engineer created a mechanical "robot" powered by ropes and pulleys to simulate human motion.

- [ ] Gregor Mendel's Genetics: Mendel's 19th-century work on pea plants laid the foundation for the field of genetics, long before DNA was discovered.

- [ ] Archytas' Flying Pigeon: In 350 BC, Archytas, a friend of Plato, reportedly built a wooden bird that was propelled by steam and could fly.

- [ ] Elisha Gray's Telephone: He filed a patent for an electric voice transmission device, or telephone, on the same day as Alexander Graham Bell, but just a few hours too late.

- [ ] The First Vending Machine: In the 1st century AD, Hero of Alexandria also created a machine that dispensed holy water after inserting a coin.

- [ ] Early Seismoscope: Zhang Heng, an ancient Chinese astronomer, invented a seismoscope in 132 AD that could indicate the direction of distant earthquakes.

- [ ] Abbas ibn Firnas' Flying Attempts: In the 9th century, this Andalusian polymath created a glider, and reportedly conducted one of the first attempts at human flight.

- [ ] The Mechanical Turk: Invented in the 18th century, this was a fake chess-playing machine that amazed audiences, though it was secretly operated by a human inside.

- [ ] Heron's Automatic Theater: Created in ancient Greece, this was a machine that used ropes, drums, and levers to perform an entire play, almost like a programmable robot.

- [ ] Conrad Gessner's Tablet: In the 16th century, Swiss scientist Gessner imagined a tablet that could store extensive information, resembling today's digital tablets.

- [ ] The Dam Buster Bomb: Invented by Barnes Wallis during WWII, this bouncing bomb was designed to skip over water and destroy German dams, an innovative idea for its time.

Funny Aviation Facts

- [ ] Wright Brothers' First Flight: The Wright Brothers' first successful flight in 1903 lasted only 12 seconds and covered just 120 feet - shorter than the length of a Boeing 747!

- [ ] Square Windows: Early airplanes had square windows, but this design caused crashes due to air pressure. The windows were redesigned to be round, solving the problem.

- [ ] Pilot and Co-pilot's Meals: Pilots and co-pilots are often required to eat different meals to avoid the risk of both becoming ill from food poisoning.

- [ ] The Black Box Isn't Black: The flight recorder, commonly known as the black box, is actually bright orange to make it easier to find after a crash.

- [ ] Paper Planes: The world record for the longest flight by a paper plane is over 226 feet, about the length of five school buses!

☐ In-Flight Lightning: Airplanes are struck by lightning frequently, but modern aircraft are designed to withstand it without any serious consequences.

☐ The Concorde's Speed: The Concorde, a supersonic passenger jet, could fly from London to New York in just under 3 hours, faster than the time zone difference.

☐ Tiny Holes in Windows: Airplane windows have a tiny hole in them, called a bleed hole, which helps regulate cabin pressure and prevent the windows from fogging up.

☐ Sleeping Pilots: On long flights, pilots are allowed to take turns napping to ensure they remain alert.

☐ The 747's Spiral Staircase: The Boeing 747 was originally designed with a spiral staircase leading to the upper deck, giving it a unique feature.

☐ The Longest Flight: The world's longest non-stop flight is from Singapore to Newark, covering about 9,534 miles in nearly 19 hours.

☐ Gigantic Fuel Tanks: A large passenger jet can use up to 1 gallon of fuel every second – over the course of a 10-hour flight, it might burn 36,000 gallons.

☐ Winglets for Efficiency: The curved wingtips on many planes, known as winglets, are designed to improve fuel efficiency and reduce drag.

☐ Tiny Tires Taking the Weight: Airplane tires are incredibly tough. They can handle the weight of an airplane landing at over 150 miles per hour.

- [ ] Faster Than the Speed of Sound: The fastest manned airplane, the X-15, flew at Mach 6.7, over six times the speed of sound.

- [ ] Floating Doors: The doors of an airplane can't be opened mid-flight due to the pressure difference inside and outside the cabin.

- [ ] The Mile-High Club: There's an unofficial 'club' known as the Mile-High Club, for people who claim to have been intimate on an airplane.

- [ ] No Parachutes on Commercial Flights: Contrary to what some may think, commercial airplanes don't carry parachutes for passengers.

- [ ] The Autopilot Myth: While planes have autopilot, pilots are constantly monitoring and adjusting the flight path, and take over for takeoff and landing.

- [ ] Low Humidity: The humidity in an airplane is lower than in some deserts, which is why you might feel dehydrated during flights.

Funny Ship Facts

- [ ] The Titanic Had Its Own Newspaper: The RMS Titanic had its own onboard newspaper, the "Atlantic Daily Bulletin," printed every day with news, advertisements, and stock prices.

- [ ] Ghost Ships: The Mary Celeste is a famous ghost ship found abandoned with everything intact. The crew's mysterious disappearance remains unsolved.

- [ ] Colorful Pirate Ships: Pirate ships were often brightly painted and had fearsome flags to intimidate their targets and make themselves more recognizable.

- [ ] A City on Water: The world's largest cruise ship, Symphony of the Seas, is like a floating city with a park, water slides, ice rink, and over 20 restaurants.

- [ ] Cats on Ships: Cats were commonly kept on ships for centuries to catch mice and rats, and were also believed to bring good luck.

- [ ] Floating Post Offices: Some ships, like the RMS Queen Mary 2, have their own postal ZIP code and post office, where you can send postcards from the middle of the ocean.

- [ ] The Speed of Sailboats: The fastest sailboats can travel over 50 knots (about 57.5 mph), almost as fast as some land vehicles.

- [ ] Ice Cream on Navy Ships: US Navy ships often carry enough ice cream to serve each sailor a scoop per day for the entire duration of the mission.

- [ ] Ship Biscuits: Old sailing ships had 'hard tack' biscuits as a staple part of the diet. They were so hard they often had to be soaked in liquid before eating.

- [ ] The Ship's Bell: The bell on a ship is traditionally used to mark the time and regulate sailors' duty watches.

- [ ] Floating Laboratories: Many modern ships are equipped as floating laboratories for oceanographic research, complete with high-tech equipment.

- [ ] Ancient Rafts: One of the earliest types of watercraft, rafts made of logs or reeds, were used 8,000 years ago.

- [ ] Ship Superstitions: It's considered bad luck to change the name of a boat or ship, according to maritime superstition.

- [ ] The Unsinkable Ship: The Unsinkable Sam was a cat that survived the sinking of three separate ships during World War II.

- [ ] Ships in Bottles: The art of putting ships in bottles started over 200 years ago. The ship is built outside the bottle and then inserted through the neck.

- [ ] Underwater Music: Some modern luxury cruise ships have underwater speakers that let you listen to music while swimming or diving.

- [ ] The Jolly Roger: The classic pirate flag with a skull and crossbones is known as the Jolly Roger. Each pirate had a unique design.

- [ ] The First Steamboat: The first successful steamboat was built by Robert Fulton in 1807, named the North River Steamboat, later known as the Clermont.

- [ ] Life Below Water: Many modern submarines have the ability to stay submerged for months, creating their own oxygen and fresh water.

- [ ] The Viking Longships: Viking longships were highly versatile, able to navigate oceans, rivers, and even small streams. They were fast, light, and had a shallow draft.

Funny Train Facts

- [ ] Fastest Trains in the World: Japan's bullet trains, or Shinkansen, can travel up to 320 km/h (200 mph), almost as fast as some racing cars!

☐ The First Steam Locomotive: The first full-scale working railway steam locomotive was built in the UK in 1804 by Richard Trevithick, a British engineer.

☐ Longest Train Journey: The Trans-Siberian Railway is the longest in the world, stretching over 9,289 kilometers (5,772 miles) from Moscow to Vladivostok.

☐ Choo Choo Sound: The classic "choo choo" sound of old steam locomotives comes from the steam being released from the engine's pistons.

☐ The Underground Railroad: This wasn't a real railroad but a network of secret routes and safe houses used by enslaved African Americans to escape to free states and Canada in the 19th century.

☐ Dining Cars: Luxury trains in the early 1900s had opulent dining cars with gourmet meals, making dining on a train a grand experience.

☐ The Longest Train: The longest train ever recorded was in Australia. In 2001, it stretched for 7.353 kilometers (4.568 miles) with 682 loaded iron ore wagons.

☐ Trains and Time Zones: The need for standardized time came from trains, as different cities had different local times, making train schedules chaotic before time zones were established.

☐ Animal-Powered Trains: Before steam and electric trains, there were horse-powered railways where horses pulled carts on tracks.

☐ The Orient Express: Famous for luxury and intrigue, this train ran from Paris to Istanbul and was the setting for Agatha Christie's novel "Murder on the Orient Express."

- ☐ Train Tracks in the UK: The UK has enough railway tracks to circle the Earth, with over 40,000 kilometers (about 25,000 miles) of track.

- ☐ The Station Cat: Some train stations in Japan have stationmaster cats, who wear uniforms and greet passengers!

- ☐ Train Roundhouses: Roundhouses are circular buildings used for storing and servicing trains, with a turntable in the center to rotate them.

- ☐ India's Lifeline: Indian Railways is one of the world's largest employers, with over 1.3 million employees, and is crucial to the country's transportation.

- ☐ The Ghost Train: The Silverpilen (Silver Arrow) in Stockholm's metro is a silver train rumored to be a ghost train, appearing suddenly and transporting passengers to abandoned stations.

- ☐ The Double-Decker Train: In some countries, trains have two levels, called double-decker trains, to carry more passengers.

- ☐ The Hogwarts Express: This fictional train in the "Harry Potter" series runs between London and the magical school Hogwarts, boarding from the hidden Platform 9 ¾.

- ☐ Toy Trains: The first toy trains appeared in the 19th century. Today, model train collecting and building is a popular hobby around the world.

- ☐ The Ghan: Australia's The Ghan, a passenger train, travels through the heart of the Australian outback, offering breathtaking views of the desert landscape.

☐ The Train Ferry: Train ferries were used to transport trains across bodies of water before bridges were built, literally ships carrying whole trains on board.

Funny Car Facts

☐ The First Car Accident: The world's first car accident occurred in 1891 in Ohio. It involved a single car and a tree, proving that you don't need traffic for accidents!

☐ Multi-Color Cars: In the early days of automobiles, cars weren't all black. They were available in various colors until Ford's assembly line made black the most common color due to faster drying paint.

☐ Flying Cars in Movies: Flying cars have been a dream for decades, featured in movies like "Back to the Future." Real prototypes exist today, but they're not quite ready for traffic!

☐ Banana Car: There's a car shaped like a banana. It's 23 feet long and was created by Steve Braithwaite as a fun art project.

☐ Horsepower: The term 'horsepower' comes from James Watt, who used it to compare the power of steam engines to draft horses. One unit of horsepower is roughly equivalent to the power of one horse.

☐ Car Radio: The first car radio wasn't introduced until about 1920. Before that, you'd have to sing to yourself for in-car entertainment!

☐ Carriages Without Horses: Early automobiles were called "horseless carriages" because people didn't have a word for a car yet.

☐ Inflatable Cars: In the 1950s, Goodyear made an inflatable car. It was never mass-produced, but it could be packed in a suitcase!

☐ The Smallest Car: The Peel P50, manufactured in the 1960s, holds the record for the smallest ever car. It's only 54 inches long and 41 inches wide!

☐ License Plates: The first cars didn't have license plates. The first plate appeared in France in 1893, followed by the Netherlands, which issued the first numbered plates.

☐ Cars on the Moon: There are three cars on the Moon left by astronauts from the Apollo 15, 16, and 17 missions. They're called Lunar Rovers.

☐ Car Horns: The first car horns weren't electric; they were mechanical and sounded like a bicycle horn.

☐ Heated Seats: The first heated car seats were introduced by Cadillac in 1966. It was a luxury feature then but is quite common now.

☐ Cars with Wood: The Ford Model T, one of the first mass-produced cars, had parts made from wood, including the frame, wheels, and dashboard.

☐ The Talking Car: In the 1980s, some cars like the Chrysler New Yorker talked to the driver, saying things like "Your door is ajar" (meaning it's open).

☐ Windshield Wipers: Windshield wipers were invented by Mary Anderson in 1903, after she saw a streetcar driver struggling to see in the rain.

☐ Cars in Space: Elon Musk's Tesla Roadster was sent into space in 2018, making it the first car to orbit the sun.

- [ ] Electric Cars in the 1800s: Electric cars aren't new; they were actually quite popular in the late 1800s and early 1900s before gasoline cars became dominant.

- [ ] Self-Driving Cars: Self-driving cars are being developed today, aiming to make driving easier and safer. But they're still learning to understand the unpredictable nature of roads.

- [ ] The 27-Liter Car: The 1932 Bugatti Type 41 Royale had a massive 12.7-liter engine. For comparison, most cars today have engines around 2 liters.

Funny Tech Trivia

- [ ] The First Computer: The first electronic digital computer, ENIAC, weighed about 27 tons – as heavy as four elephants, and took up an entire room.

- [ ] The Origin of 'Bug': The term 'bug' in computing came from a real moth found in a computer by Grace Hopper in the 1940s. It was causing malfunctions, hence 'debugging'.

- [ ] Wi-Fi's Strange Beginnings: Wi-Fi technology was developed from a failed experiment to detect mini black holes. It's now used worldwide for wireless internet access.

- [ ] First Computer Mouse: The first computer mouse was made of wood, created in 1964 by Douglas Engelbart. It looked quite different from today's sleek plastic models.

- [ ] Domain Name Rush: The first-ever domain name registered was symbolics.com on March 15, 1985. Now, millions of domain names are registered.

☐ The Y2K Bug: The year 2000 caused panic as people thought computers would malfunction by not recognizing '00' as 2000, but 1900. Spoiler: The world didn't end!

☐ Email Predates the Internet: Email was created in 1971, even before the internet was fully developed. It's been a crucial part of our online life ever since.

☐ Mobile Phone Evolution: The first mobile phone, released in 1983, was about the size of a brick and cost almost $4,000.

☐ The First Smartphone: IBM's Simon Personal Communicator, released in 1994, was the first smartphone. It combined a mobile phone with a PDA (Personal Digital Assistant).

☐ Google's Original Name: Google was initially named 'BackRub' in 1996, named for its method of analyzing the web's 'back links'.

☐ Computer Viruses: The first computer virus was created in the early 1970s, named the Creeper virus, which displayed the message, "I'm the creeper, catch me if you can!"

☐ World's First Webcam: The first webcam was used in Cambridge to monitor a coffee pot, saving people a wasted trip to an empty coffee pot!

☐ Texting Abbreviations are Old: Texting abbreviations like 'LOL' are often seen as modern, but they've been around since the 1980s.

☐ Emoji Language: The first emoji were created in 1999 in Japan. They've evolved into a universal digital language for expressing emotions.

☐ First YouTube Video: The first video uploaded to
YouTube in 2005 was titled "Me at the zoo." It was an
18-second clip and is still viewable today.

☐ The First Computer Virus for Windows: Named
'WinVer 1.4', it was harmless and designed only to
spread and display a message.

☐ Twitter's Character Limit: Twitter's 140-character limit
was originally set to fit into a single SMS message,
which had a 160-character limit.

☐ Internet in Space: The International Space Station
got its own internet connection in 2010, allowing
astronauts to browse the web.

☐ Quantum Computing: Quantum computers use
quantum bits or 'qubits', which can exist in multiple
states at once, potentially allowing them to solve
complex problems much faster than classical
computers.

☐ Social Media's Rapid Growth: Facebook reached 1
billion users in 8 years, while it took television 13
years to reach that many viewers.

Mythical Beasts

☐ Unicorns in Scotland: The unicorn is Scotland's
national animal, symbolizing purity, innocence, and
power in Celtic mythology.

☐ Dragons Across Cultures: Dragons are found in
myths worldwide, from the fire-breathing beasts of
European folklore to the wise and benevolent
dragons of Chinese legend.

☐ Bigfoot's Big Feet: Bigfoot, also known as Sasquatch, is a legendary creature in North American folklore, described as a large, hairy, ape-like being with notably large feet.

☐ The Loch Ness Monster: Nessie, the famous creature said to inhabit Scotland's Loch Ness, is often depicted as a long-necked creature with one or more humps protruding from the water.

☐ The Kraken: This giant sea monster from Norse mythology is said to dwell off the coasts of Norway and Greenland, terrorizing sailors with its enormous size.

☐ Mermaids and Their Songs: In many myths, mermaids are known for their enchanting voices, luring sailors to their doom with their beautiful singing.

☐ Centaurs' Dual Nature: In Greek mythology, centaurs, creatures with the upper body of a human and the lower body of a horse, represent the dual nature of humanity – both civilized and wild.

☐ The Phoenix's Rebirth: The phoenix, a bird from Greek mythology, is said to live for hundreds of years before bursting into flames and then being reborn from its ashes.

☐ Elves' Pointy Ears: In folklore, elves are often depicted with pointy ears, symbolizing their connection with nature and their magical powers.

☐ Vampires and Garlic: In folklore, vampires, creatures that drink blood to survive, are said to be repelled by garlic, a trait that has become a popular trope in vampire stories.

☐ The Chimera's Three Heads: In Greek mythology, the Chimera is a monstrous fire-breathing creature, typically depicted with the heads of a lion, a goat, and a serpent.

☐ Cyclops' Single Eye: Cyclopes are giant creatures from Greek mythology with a single eye in the middle of their forehead, known for their strength and skill in blacksmithing.

☐ Werewolves and Full Moons: Werewolves, mythological humans with the ability to transform into wolves, are commonly associated with the full moon, though this connection is mostly a modern invention.

☐ The Yeti of the Himalayas: Also known as the Abominable Snowman, the Yeti is said to be an ape-like creature taller than an average human, living in the Himalayan mountains.

☐ Goblins' Mischief: Goblins are small, mischievous creatures from European folklore, often causing trouble for humans with their pranks.

☐ Banshees' Wails: In Irish legend, a banshee is a female spirit who heralds the death of a family member by wailing or shrieking.

☐ The Minotaur's Labyrinth: In Greek mythology, the Minotaur, a creature with the head of a bull and the body of a man, dwelt in the center of a complex maze called the Labyrinth.

☐ Leprechauns and Gold: In Irish folklore, leprechauns are small, bearded men who partake in mischief, and are often associated with a pot of gold at the end of a rainbow.

- ☐ Hydra's Regenerating Heads: The Hydra, a serpentine water monster from Greek mythology, had multiple heads – when one was cut off, two more would grow back in its place.

- ☐ The Basilisk, King of Serpents: In European legends, the basilisk, known as the king of serpents, could cause death with a single glance.

Legendary Mythical Heroes

- ☐ Hercules and His Twelve Labors: Hercules, a hero from Greek mythology, is famous for his incredible strength and for completing twelve near-impossible labors, including fighting the nine-headed Hydra.

- ☐ Achilles' Heel: Achilles, a Greek hero of the Trojan War, was invulnerable except for his heel. Today, an "Achilles' heel" refers to someone's single point of vulnerability.

- ☐ King Arthur and the Round Table: King Arthur, a legendary British leader, had a famous round table where he and his knights would gather, symbolizing equality among them.

- ☐ Odysseus' Odyssey: Odysseus, the king of Ithaca, took 10 years to return home after the Trojan War. His journey, full of adventures and challenges, is known as "The Odyssey."

- ☐ Thor's Hammer: In Norse mythology, Thor, the god of thunder, had a powerful hammer called Mjölnir, which always returned to his hand after being thrown.

- ☐ Robin Hood and His Merry Men: Robin Hood, a heroic outlaw from English folklore, is known for "robbing from the rich and giving to the poor," along with his band of Merry Men.

☐ The Mighty Beowulf: Beowulf, a hero of the Geats, is the protagonist of one of the oldest surviving pieces of literature in the English language. He fought and defeated the monster Grendel.

☐ Theseus and the Minotaur: Theseus, a founder-hero of Athens, bravely entered the Labyrinth and defeated the Minotaur, a creature half-man, half-bull.

☐ Perseus and Medusa: In Greek mythology, Perseus beheaded Medusa, the Gorgon with snakes for hair whose gaze could turn people to stone.

☐ Gilgamesh's Epic: Gilgamesh, a Sumerian hero-king, is the subject of one of the earliest works of literature, where he embarks on a quest for immortality.

☐ Jason and the Golden Fleece: Jason, a hero in Greek mythology, led the Argonauts in a quest for the Golden Fleece, a symbol of authority and kingship.

☐ The Valkyries of Norse Mythology: The Valkyries, in Norse legend, were female figures who chose those who may die in battle and those who may live.

☐ Cu Chulainn's Warp Spasm: In Irish mythology, Cu Chulainn, a legendary warrior, underwent a terrifying transformation known as a 'warp spasm,' making him an unstoppable force in battle.

☐ Bellerophon and Pegasus: Bellerophon, a hero in Greek mythology, tamed the winged horse Pegasus and defeated the monstrous Chimera.

☐ Samson's Hair: In the biblical story, Samson's incredible strength was in his hair, and he lost it when Delilah had his hair cut while he was asleep.

☐ Siegfried and the Dragon: In Germanic mythology, Siegfried heroically defeated a dragon, bathing in its blood to become invincible.

☐ Finn McCool and the Giant's Causeway: According to Irish legend, Finn McCool built the Giant's Causeway to walk to Scotland to fight another giant.

☐ The Legend of Mulan: Mulan, a legendary figure from Chinese folklore, disguised herself as a man to take her father's place in the army.

☐ The Labors of Rostam: In Persian mythology, Rostam is a hero known for his extraordinary strength, courage, and loyalty, and is featured in the epic 'Shahnameh.'

☐ The Adventures of Sun Wukong: Sun Wukong, also known as the Monkey King in Chinese mythology, possesses immense strength, speed, and magical powers, including the ability to transform into various animals and objects.

Mythical Origin Tales

☐ Norse Creation Myth: In Norse mythology, the world started from a void named Ginnungagap. The first beings were the frost giant Ymir and the cow Audhumla.

☐ Greek Chaos and Cosmos: According to Greek mythology, in the beginning, there was only Chaos. From Chaos emerged Gaia (Earth), Tartarus (the Underworld), and Eros (Love), who brought order to the universe.

- [ ] Egyptian Sun God, Ra: In Egyptian mythology, Ra, the sun god, emerged from the chaos at the beginning of time and created all forms of life.

- [ ] Hindu Cosmic Egg: Hindus believe the universe originated from a cosmic egg. From this egg emerged the gods, humans, and all of existence.

- [ ] Chinese Giant, Pangu: According to Chinese myth, the universe began as an egg. A giant named Pangu hatched from it and formed the Earth and sky from the egg's parts.

- [ ] Aboriginal Dreamtime: Australian Aboriginals believe in 'Dreamtime,' where ancestral beings emerged from the earth and sky to create life and important landmarks.

- [ ] Yoruba Myth: In Yoruba mythology, the god Orisha-nla was sent by the supreme deity, Olorun, to create the earth and humanity.

- [ ] Polynesian Island Creation: Polynesian myths say that the god Maui fished the islands from the sea with a magical hook.

- [ ] Aztec Five Suns: The Aztecs believed the world was created and destroyed in cycles by different sun gods. We are currently living under the fifth sun.

- [ ] Mayan Maize God: The Mayan creation story includes the Maize God, who died and from whose body corn, a staple of their diet, sprang.

- [ ] Norse World Tree, Yggdrasil: In Norse mythology, the universe is structured around Yggdrasil, the World Tree, connecting various realms like Asgard and Midgard.

- Iroquois Turtle Island: The Iroquois believe the world began with Earth being formed on the back of a giant turtle.

- Japanese Sun Goddess, Amaterasu: In Japanese Shinto belief, the universe was created by the gods Izanagi and Izanami. The sun goddess, Amaterasu, is their descendant.

- Hopi Spider Woman: The Hopi tribe believes in Spider Woman, Tawa, who wove the world into existence.

- Finnish Kalevala: The Finnish epic 'Kalevala' describes the Earth forming from the shards of a duck egg and the sky as the egg's upper half.

- Greek Titan Atlas: After the Titans' defeat, Atlas was condemned to hold up the sky for eternity, separating it from the Earth.

- Biblical Genesis: In the Judeo-Christian creation story, God created the world in six days, resting on the seventh.

- Norse Ice and Fire: In Norse mythology, the world was created from the interaction of fire from Muspelheim and ice from Niflheim.

- The Rainbow Serpent: In many Australian Aboriginal cultures, the Rainbow Serpent is a key part of creation myths, shaping the landscape and creating life.

- Viking Midgard: According to Norse legend, humans live in Midgard, a world created from the body of the slain giant Ymir.

Funny Mythical Tales

- ☐ Hercules' Fashion Faux Pas: As part of his twelve labors, Hercules had to clean the Augean stables. He redirected a river to do the job, showing brains over brawn and probably staying very far from the smell.

- ☐ Dionysus' Dolphin Ride: Dionysus, the Greek god of wine, once turned a group of pirates who captured him into dolphins after they refused to believe he was a god.

- ☐ Apollo's Flawed Love Life: The Greek god Apollo was struck by Cupid's arrow, causing him to fall in love with Daphne. Daphne, not interested, transformed into a laurel tree to escape his advances.

- ☐ Thor's Dress-Up: In Norse mythology, Thor once dressed as a bride to trick a giant and recover his stolen hammer, Mjölnir.

- ☐ Baldur's Invincibility: Baldur, a Norse god, was invincible to everything except mistletoe. His mother asked everything in the world not to harm him but forgot about mistletoe.

- ☐ The Greek God of Ugliness: Hephaestus, the Greek god of blacksmiths, was considered the ugliest of the gods, yet he married Aphrodite, the goddess of beauty.

- ☐ Eris' Golden Apple: Eris, the Greek goddess of discord, wasn't invited to a wedding, so she tossed a golden apple inscribed "To the fairest one," sparking a vanity-fueled dispute among goddesses.

- ☐ Pan's Panic: Pan, the Greek god of the wild, had a habit of yelling suddenly to scare travelers, giving us the word 'panic.'

- [ ] The Monkey King's Rebellion: In Chinese mythology, Sun Wukong, the Monkey King, rebelled against heaven, stole the peaches of immortality, and fought an army of gods.

- [ ] Odin's Wisdom: Odin, the Norse king of gods, sacrificed one of his eyes in exchange for wisdom. He apparently didn't see that coming.

- [ ] Set and Horus' Lettuce Incident: In Egyptian mythology, Set attempted to discredit Horus by claiming to have dominated him. Horus proved him wrong with a trick involving lettuce, Set's favorite food.

- [ ] Narcissus' Self-Obsession: Narcissus, in Greek mythology, was so enamored with his reflection in water that he fell in and drowned, leading to the term 'narcissism.'

- [ ] Anansi's Stories: Anansi, the African trickster spider, obtained the rights to all stories by tricking the sky god with clever, yet humorous challenges.

- [ ] Loki's Bald Mistake: Loki mischievously cut off the hair of Thor's wife, Sif. To avoid Thor's wrath, he had to replace it with magical hair made by dwarfs.

- [ ] The Turtles All the Way Down: A famous anecdote involves a scientist explaining the earth orbiting the sun, and an old lady retorting that the world is a flat disk on the back of a giant turtle, and it's "turtles all the way down."

- [ ] Achelous' Shape-Shifting Battle: In Greek mythology, the river god Achelous lost a shape-shifting battle to Hercules and turned into the horn that became the Cornucopia, the horn of plenty.

☐ Arachne's Weaving Contest: Arachne, a mortal, boasted she was a better weaver than Athena. Athena turned her into a spider for her hubris – the first 'spider woman.'

☐ The Pied Piper's Revenge: In the legend of the Pied Piper, when not paid for ridding Hamelin of rats, he lured away the town's children with his music.

☐ Janus' Two Faces: Janus, the Roman god of beginnings, had two faces – one looking to the future and one to the past, symbolizing his understanding of both.

Magical Artifacts

☐ The Golden Fleece: In Greek mythology, the Golden Fleece was a golden-wooled ram's fleece, a symbol of authority and kingship, and the quest for it formed the basis of the Argonauts' expedition.

☐ Thor's Hammer, Mjölnir: In Norse mythology, Mjölnir was the powerful hammer wielded by Thor, capable of leveling mountains and always returning to the owner's hand.

☐ The Philosopher's Stone: Fabled to turn base metals into gold and grant eternal life, the Philosopher's Stone is a legendary alchemical substance.

☐ Pandora's Box: In Greek mythology, Pandora's Box wasn't actually a box but a jar containing all the world's evils. When opened, it released them, leaving only hope inside.

☐ Aladdin's Lamp: From Middle Eastern folklore, Aladdin's Lamp housed a genie who could grant the owner's wishes, symbolizing the unexpected and immense power.

☐ The Holy Grail: In Christian mythology, the Holy Grail is the cup that Jesus drank from at the Last Supper, said to have miraculous powers.

☐ Flying Carpets: Found in many Eastern stories, these magical carpets can transport their riders swiftly and smoothly through the air.

☐ Hermes' Winged Sandals: In Greek mythology, these sandals carried the messenger god Hermes, and anyone who wore them, at incredible speeds.

☐ The Mirror of Erised: From the "Harry Potter" series, this mirror shows the deepest and most desperate desire of one's heart.

☐ The Sword in the Stone: Another legendary item from Arthurian tales, only the rightful king of Britain could pull this sword from its stone.

☐ The Cornucopia: Also known as the Horn of Plenty, it was a magical horn in Greek mythology that provided an endless supply of food and drink.

☐ Cupid's Bow and Arrows: In Roman mythology, Cupid's arrows could make anyone fall in love, with the golden arrow inciting love and the lead one repelling it.

☐ The Cloak of Invisibility: A common item in folklore and fairy tales, this cloak renders the wearer invisible to others.

☐ The Ring of Gyges: From Plato's story, this ring could make the wearer invisible, leading to discussions about morality and power.

- [ ] The Cintamani Stone: In Buddhist and Hindu mythology, this wish-fulfilling jewel is a powerful artifact and a symbol of the bestowal of divine favor.

- [ ] Poseidon's Trident: In Greek mythology, this three-pronged spear was wielded by the god of the sea, Poseidon, and it could control water and cause earthquakes.

- [ ] The Apple of Discord: This golden apple inscribed "To the Fairest" sparked a vanity-fueled dispute among goddesses, leading to the Trojan War in Greek mythology.

- [ ] The Sampo: In Finnish mythology, the Sampo was a magical artifact that brought its owner good fortune and prosperity.

- [ ] The Book of Thoth: In Egyptian mythology, this book offered knowledge of magic and the power to understand animals and spirits, but it was perilously guarded.

Nature's Extremes

- [ ] The Eye of the Hurricane: The center of a hurricane, known as the eye, is eerily calm compared to the storm's outer parts, with clear skies and lower wind speeds.

- [ ] Richter Scale for Earthquakes: The Richter scale, developed in 1935, measures earthquake magnitudes. Each increase by 1 point means the quake is 10 times stronger!

- [ ] Tsunamis Travel Fast: Tsunamis can travel as fast as a jet plane, up to 500 mph (800 km/h), across the open ocean, due to the enormous energy released by the underwater disturbance.

☐ Lightning in Volcanic Eruptions: Amazingly, volcanic eruptions can produce spectacular lightning, caused by the collision of ash particles in the eruption plume.

☐ The Tornado Alley: In the USA, there's an area called "Tornado Alley" in the Midwest known for frequent tornadoes due to the collision of cold and warm air.

☐ Underwater Earthquakes: Most tsunamis are caused by underwater earthquakes, which displace massive amounts of water, creating powerful waves.

☐ The Saffir-Simpson Hurricane Scale: Hurricanes are categorized from 1 to 5 based on wind speed, with 5 being the most destructive.

☐ Earthquake-proof Buildings: In earthquake-prone areas like Japan, buildings are designed to absorb seismic waves, making them shake less and reducing damage.

☐ The Ring of Fire: The Pacific Ring of Fire is a horseshoe-shaped area with a high number of earthquakes and volcanic eruptions, caused by tectonic plate movements.

☐ Largest Recorded Earthquake: The largest recorded earthquake struck Chile in 1960 with a magnitude of 9.5.

☐ Hurricane Names: Hurricanes are named alphabetically from a list predetermined by the World Meteorological Organization. Each year the list of names rotates.

☐ Tsunami Warning Systems: After the 2004 Indian Ocean tsunami, many countries installed deep-sea buoys that detect tsunamis early, providing vital warning time.

- [ ] Tornadoes' Mysterious Paths: Tornadoes can change direction suddenly and can even backtrack, making them highly unpredictable and dangerous.

- [ ] The Power of a Hurricane: A large hurricane can release the energy equivalent to 10 atomic bombs per second.

- [ ] Earth's Moving Plates: Earthquakes happen because Earth's surface is made of tectonic plates that constantly move and sometimes clash.

- [ ] Volcano Lightning: Known as a "dirty thunderstorm," the lightning in a volcanic eruption is a spectacular sight and results from the static charge of particles in the volcanic ash.

- [ ] Supercell Storms: Supercells are the most severe type of thunderstorm, capable of producing violent tornadoes, massive hailstones, and flash flooding.

- [ ] Sand Hurricanes on Mars: Mars experiences dust storms that are much like Earth's hurricanes, covering huge areas and lasting for weeks.

- [ ] Seismic Sea Waves: Tsunamis, also called seismic sea waves, aren't like normal ocean waves caused by the wind but are generated by seismic activity.

- [ ] Quicksand During Earthquakes: During an earthquake, water-saturated sand can lose its strength and behave more like a liquid, a phenomenon known as soil liquefaction.

Weather Phenomena

- [ ] Ball Lightning: A rare form of lightning that appears as glowing, spherical objects which can float in the air. They are unpredictable and have baffled scientists for years.

- ☐ Catatumbo Lightning: In Venezuela, there's a place where lightning strikes almost continuously. The Catatumbo lightning occurs for up to 160 nights a year, 10 hours per day.

- ☐ Rain of Animals: Sometimes, small animals like frogs or fish get swept up in waterspouts and fall from the sky during rainstorms.

- ☐ St. Elmo's Fire: This weather phenomenon creates a bright blue or violet glow, appearing like fire in the sky, usually during thunderstorms.

- ☐ Halos Around the Sun or Moon: Caused by ice crystals in the atmosphere, halos are beautiful rings that can appear around the sun or moon.

- ☐ Auroras: The Northern and Southern Lights are natural light displays in the Earth's sky, predominantly seen in high-latitude regions. They're caused by solar winds disturbing the magnetosphere.

- ☐ Mammatus Clouds: These clouds look like a field of cotton balls hanging from the sky and usually form after severe thunderstorms.

- ☐ The Morning Glory Clouds: A rare type of rolling cloud that can be seen in Northern Australia. These long, tube-shaped clouds can stretch up to 1,000 kilometers long.

- ☐ Lenticular Clouds: These stationary, lens-shaped clouds often form near mountains and have been mistaken for UFOs due to their appearance.

- ☐ Supercell Thunderstorms: These are the largest type of thunderstorms and can give birth to the most dangerous tornadoes.

- [ ] Heat Bursts: After thunderstorms, temperatures can rise dramatically in a short period, creating what's known as a heat burst.

- [ ] Virga: This phenomenon looks like trails of rain hanging under a cloud and evaporating before hitting the ground.

- [ ] Sun Dogs: Bright spots that appear on both sides of the sun, usually in a halo. Sun dogs are caused by the refraction of sunlight passing through ice crystals in the atmosphere.

- [ ] Snow Donuts: Under specific conditions, wind can blow chunks of snow to create large, donut-shaped snow rolls.

- [ ] Fire Whirls: Also known as fire tornadoes or fire devils, these are whirlwinds induced by fire and often composed of flame or ash.

- [ ] Fog Bows: Similar to rainbows, fog bows appear in fog rather than rain and are much fainter and whiter due to the smaller water droplets.

- [ ] Blood Rain: Rain that appears red in color, typically caused by dust or sand particles from deserts mixing with water in clouds.

- [ ] Diamond Dust: A ground-level cloud composed of tiny ice crystals. It's often seen in polar regions and can create halos.

- [ ] Thundersnow: A rare kind of thunderstorm with snow falling as the primary precipitation instead of rain.

- [ ] Moonbows: Similar to rainbows, but produced by light reflected off the surface of the moon rather than direct sunlight, hence appearing much fainter.

Volcanoes

- [ ] The Tallest Volcano: Mauna Loa in Hawaii is the world's largest volcano in terms of volume and area covered. It rises over 4 km above sea level but extends about 5 km below sea level.

- [ ] Volcanic Lightning: During eruptions, volcanoes can produce spectacular lightning, known as volcanic lightning or "dirty thunderstorms," caused by the collision of ash particles.

- [ ] The Ring of Fire: Most of the world's volcanoes are part of the Ring of Fire, a major area in the Pacific Ocean where a large number of earthquakes and volcanic eruptions occur.

- [ ] Underwater Volcanoes: There are more volcanoes underwater than on land. These submarine volcanoes can form new islands when their eruptions break the ocean's surface.

- [ ] The Loudest Sound: The eruption of Krakatoa in Indonesia in 1883 is considered the loudest sound ever recorded. It was heard as far away as 3,000 miles.

- [ ] Olympus Mons on Mars: The largest volcano in the solar system is not on Earth, but on Mars. Olympus Mons stands about 13 miles high and 370 miles wide.

- [ ] Yellowstone's Supervolcano: Yellowstone National Park sits on a huge volcanic hotspot. The supervolcano there has had three massive eruptions in the past, with intervals of about 600,000 to 800,000 years.

- ☐ Lava Lakes: Some volcanoes contain lava lakes, which are large volumes of molten lava, often contained in a crater or broad depression.

- ☐ The Fastest Lava: In 1959, Kilauea Iki erupted in Hawaii, producing lava fountains up to 1,900 feet. The lava flows were measured at speeds of up to 60 km/h.

- ☐ Volcanic Ash: Volcanic ash can travel hundreds of miles and affect climate patterns. It's made of tiny fragments of jagged rock, minerals, and volcanic glass.

- ☐ Pompeii's Fate: In 79 AD, Mount Vesuvius erupted, burying the city of Pompeii under a thick carpet of volcanic ash, preserving it for centuries.

- ☐ Lava Tubes: These are natural conduits formed by flowing lava which moves beneath the hardened surface of a lava flow, often forming caves after the lava flows out.

- ☐ Volcano Eruptions and Climate Change: Large volcanic eruptions can affect the Earth's climate. The ash and sulfur dioxide can lower temperatures globally.

- ☐ Volcanic Islands: Islands like Hawaii and Iceland were formed by volcanic eruptions that occurred over thousands of years.

- ☐ The Deadliest Volcano: The eruption of Tambora in Indonesia in 1815 is the deadliest in recorded history, causing the "Year Without a Summer" in 1816 due to the volcanic ash in the atmosphere.

- ☐ Geothermal Energy: Volcanoes can be used to produce geothermal energy, a renewable energy source.

- [ ] Pele's Hair: Named after the Hawaiian goddess of volcanoes, Pele's hair is a form of lava that cools into thin strands of volcanic glass, carried by the wind.

- [ ] Volcanic Bombs: These are large rocks thrown from an erupting volcano, which can be the size of a small car.

- [ ] Shield Volcanoes: These have gentle slopes and are formed by the eruption of low-viscosity lava that can flow a long distance.

- [ ] Acid Rain from Volcanoes: The sulfur dioxide released from volcanoes can mix with rain to form acid rain, which can harm plant and animal life.

Deserts

- [ ] The Largest Desert: The Antarctic Desert, covering the continent of Antarctica, is the largest desert in the world, even larger than the Sahara.

- [ ] Deserts Can Be Cold: Not all deserts are hot! Cold deserts, like the Gobi Desert in Asia, have snow and ice in winter.

- [ ] The Sahara's Size: The Sahara Desert in Africa covers an area almost as large as the United States or China.

- [ ] Rain in the Desert: Some deserts, like the Atacama in Chile, are so dry that they receive less than 1 inch of rain per year.

- [ ] Desert Plants: Cacti and other desert plants store water in their leaves or stems and have deep root systems to find water underground.

- ☐ Sand Dunes: Only about 20% of deserts are covered in sand. The largest sand dunes can reach heights of over 500 feet.

- ☐ The Fastest Animal: The Saharan cheetah, one of the fastest animals in the world, lives in the Sahara Desert and can run at speeds of 60 mph.

- ☐ Desert Mirages: Mirages, optical illusions of water, are common in deserts. They occur due to the refraction of light through layers of hot and cold air.

- ☐ Nighttime in the Desert: Deserts can get very cold at night because the dry air does not hold heat well.

- ☐ Flowers in the Desert: Some deserts, like the Sonoran, experience a super bloom of wildflowers covering the ground with vibrant colors after rare rainfalls.

- ☐ Oasis Ecosystems: Oases, areas of vegetation fed by natural springs, are like islands of life in the vast desert.

- ☐ Desert Rivers: Some deserts have rivers that run through them. The Nile River, for example, flows through the Sahara.

- ☐ Living Sand Dunes: Sand dunes are not static; they move and change shape due to wind patterns.

- ☐ The Singing Sands: In some deserts, sand dunes can produce sounds or 'sing' when the sand moves, a phenomenon not fully understood.

- ☐ Rocky Deserts: The Mojave Desert in North America has more rock and hard-packed dirt than sand.

☐ Desert Fog: Coastal deserts like the Namib can get fog coming in from the sea, providing moisture for unique plants and animals.

☐ Solar Power in Deserts: Deserts are ideal for solar energy production due to their sunny, clear skies and vast open spaces.

☐ Camels, the Desert Ships: Camels are perfectly adapted for desert life, with their ability to go without water for up to two weeks.

☐ Salt Flats: Some deserts have salt flats where lakes have evaporated, leaving behind vast stretches of salt.

☐ Desertification: This process turns fertile land into desert, often due to drought, deforestation, or improper agriculture practices.

Mountains

☐ The Highest Peak: Mount Everest, standing at 29,029 feet, is the highest mountain peak in the world, located in the Himalayas on the border between Nepal and Tibet.

☐ Mountains Under the Sea: There are mountains underwater too! The Hawaiian-Emperor seamount chain in the Pacific Ocean is one of the longest mountain ranges, mostly submerged.

☐ The Age of Mountains: Some of the oldest mountains in the world, like the Appalachians in North America, are over 480 million years old.

☐ Mountains on Other Planets: Mars is home to Olympus Mons, the tallest volcano in our solar system, standing at about 13.6 miles high, nearly three times the height of Mount Everest.

☐ Living on Mountains: The Andean city of La Rinconada in Peru, at over 16,700 feet, is the highest permanent settlement in the world.

☐ Mountains and Climate: As you climb a mountain, the temperature drops about 3.5°F for every 1,000 feet you go up.

☐ The Rocky Mountains: This mountain range in North America stretches more than 3,000 miles, from New Mexico in the U.S. to British Columbia in Canada.

☐ Volcanic Mountains: Some mountains are volcanoes, like Mount Fuji in Japan. They're formed from eruptions that pile up lava, ash, and rocks.

☐ The Mountain Gorillas: The endangered mountain gorillas live in the Virunga Mountains in Central Africa, one of the few places in the world where these majestic creatures can be found in the wild.

☐ The Andes: South America's Andes are the longest continental mountain range in the world, stretching for about 4,300 miles.

☐ Mountains and Rivers: Many of the world's rivers start in mountain ranges. The snow and ice melt from mountains feed these rivers.

☐ Glaciers on Mountains: Glaciers are found on mountains all around the world. These slow-moving rivers of ice shape the landscape over time.

☐ Mountain Biodiversity: Mountains are home to a wide variety of plants and animals, many of which are found nowhere else in the world.

- ☐ The Himalayas Growing: The Himalayan mountain range is still growing taller! The collision of tectonic plates causes them to rise about 1 cm per year.

- ☐ Mount Kilimanjaro's Snow: Despite being near the Equator, Mount Kilimanjaro in Tanzania is capped with snow and has glaciers.

- ☐ The Alps' Formation: The European Alps were formed about 65 million years ago when the African and Eurasian tectonic plates collided.

- ☐ Mountain Air: The air at high altitudes in mountains is thinner, which means it has less oxygen, making breathing more difficult.

- ☐ Table Mountain: Cape Town's Table Mountain in South Africa has a flat top, giving it the appearance of a table.

- ☐ Cultural Significance: Mountains hold significant cultural and religious importance in many cultures. For example, Mount Olympus in Greece was considered the home of the gods in ancient Greek mythology.

- ☐ Mountain Echoes: Sound waves can bounce off mountain surfaces, creating echoes. This natural phenomenon is often a source of fascination and fun for hikers and climbers.

Ocean Mysteries

- ☐ The Ocean's Depth: The deepest part of the ocean is the Mariana Trench in the Pacific, reaching about 36,000 feet deep, deeper than Mount Everest is tall.

- ☐ Underwater Waterfalls: The Denmark Strait underwater waterfall, between Greenland and Iceland, carries cold water down 11,500 feet, making it the world's largest waterfall, underwater or on land.

- ☐ Bioluminescent Creatures: Many deep-sea creatures produce their own light through bioluminescence, creating a beautiful underwater light show.

- ☐ The Great Barrier Reef: This is the largest living structure on Earth, so huge that it's visible from space.

- ☐ Sunken Cities: Underwater explorations have discovered ancient cities, like the Egyptian city of Thonis-Heracleion, submerged and preserved in time.

- ☐ Immense Pressure: At the deepest point of the ocean, the pressure is like having 50 jumbo jets piled on top of you.

- ☐ Brine Pools: These are underwater lakes of extremely salty water that can be toxic to marine animals, creating a surreal underwater scene.

- ☐ The Ocean's Blue Color: The ocean appears blue because water absorbs colors in the red part of the light spectrum and reflects the blue.

- ☐ More Mountains Underwater: The Earth's longest mountain range is actually underwater, called the Mid-Oceanic Ridge, spanning about 40,000 miles.

- ☐ The Mysterious Bermuda Triangle: An area in the North Atlantic Ocean, it's famous for the mysterious disappearance of ships and airplanes.

- ☐ The Lost City of Atlantis: A legendary city said to have sunk into the ocean, Atlantis has been a subject of intrigue and speculation for centuries.

- ☐ The Giant Squid: Once a mythical creature, the giant squid is very real, living deep in the ocean, and can grow up to 43 feet.

- ☐ Underwater Volcanoes: There are more volcanoes underwater than on the Earth's surface. These volcanoes can form islands when they erupt.

- ☐ The Sargasso Sea: This sea in the middle of the North Atlantic Ocean has no shores, bounded only by ocean currents.

- ☐ The Ocean's Silent Zone: The SOFAR channel, or deep sound channel, is a layer of water in the ocean where sound travels at minimal speed, allowing sounds to be carried over great distances.

- ☐ Black Smokers: These are deep-sea vents emitting jets of black, mineral-rich water, creating unique ecosystems thousands of feet below the ocean's surface.

- ☐ Coral Spawning: Once a year, many coral species release their eggs and sperm all at once in a synchronized event, turning the ocean into a colorful underwater snowstorm.

- ☐ The Ocean's "Rivers": There are massive currents underwater that move vast amounts of water around the globe, much like rivers in the ocean.

- ☐ The Ocean's Oxygen: About 50-80% of the Earth's oxygen comes from the ocean, primarily from tiny plants called phytoplankton.

☐ Hydrothermal Vents: These underwater geysers spew hot, mineral-rich water, supporting unique ecosystems with organisms that thrive in extreme conditions.

Unusual Natural Records

☐ The Oldest Living Tree: A bristlecone pine tree in California, named Methuselah, is over 4,800 years old, making it the oldest known living tree on Earth.

☐ The Tallest Waterfall: Angel Falls in Venezuela is the world's highest uninterrupted waterfall, with a height of 3,212 feet, about 15 times the height of Niagara Falls.

☐ The Deepest Lake: Lake Baikal in Siberia is the deepest lake in the world, reaching a depth of about 5,387 feet, and contains 20% of the world's fresh surface water.

☐ The Longest River: The Nile River in Africa is the longest river in the world, stretching approximately 4,132 miles.

☐ The Largest Living Organism: The Armillaria ostoyae, or honey fungus, in the Blue Mountains of Oregon, covers over 2,384 acres and is estimated to be around 2,400 years old.

☐ The Fastest Gust of Wind: The fastest wind speed ever recorded on Earth was 253 miles per hour at Australia's Barrow Island during Cyclone Olivia in 1996.

☐ The Driest Place: The Atacama Desert in Chile is the driest place on Earth. Some weather stations there have never recorded rain.

☐ The Most Electric Place: Lake Maracaibo in Venezuela experiences more lightning than any other place in the world, with an average of 260 storm days per year.

☐ The Coldest Inhabited Place: The village of Oymyakon in Siberia holds the record for the coldest permanently inhabited place on Earth, where temperatures can drop below -58°F.

☐ The Largest Flower: The Rafflesia arnoldii flower in Southeast Asia is the largest flower in the world, with blooms up to 3 feet in diameter and weighing up to 15 pounds.

☐ The Fastest Animal: The peregrine falcon is the fastest animal on Earth, reaching speeds over 200 mph during its high-speed dive.

☐ The Hottest Temperature: The highest temperature ever recorded was 134°F in Furnace Creek Ranch, Death Valley, California, in 1913.

☐ The Most Acidic Lake: The Kawah Ijen Crater Lake in Indonesia is the most acidic lake in the world, with a pH close to zero.

☐ The Brightest Bioluminescent Bay: Mosquito Bay in Vieques, Puerto Rico, is considered the brightest bioluminescent bay in the world due to the high concentration of glowing microorganisms.

☐ The Oldest Fossil: The oldest fossils on Earth are stromatolites from Australia, estimated to be around 3.48 billion years old.

☐ The Longest Cave System: Mammoth Cave in Kentucky is the world's longest known cave system, with more than 400 miles of explored passageways.

- ☐ The Largest Salt Flat: Salar de Uyuni in Bolivia is the world's largest salt flat, covering over 4,086 square miles. It's so flat and reflective, it's used to calibrate satellites.

- ☐ The Tallest Tree: The tallest tree in the world is a coast redwood named Hyperion in California, standing at 379.7 feet tall.

- ☐ The Most Isolated Tree: The Tree of Ténéré in the Sahara Desert was once considered the most isolated tree on Earth, standing alone for over 250 miles.

- ☐ The Highest Tide: The Bay of Fundy in Canada has the highest tides in the world, where the difference between low and high tide can be over 53 feet.

Fascinating Chemistry

- ☐ Bouncing Rubber Eggs: By soaking an egg in vinegar for a few days, the acetic acid dissolves the calcium carbonate shell, leaving a squishy, bouncy egg.

- ☐ Color-Changing Chemicals: Certain chemicals change color based on pH levels. Red cabbage juice, for example, turns red in acidic solutions and green in basic solutions.

- ☐ Glow-in-the-Dark Chemicals: Some substances like phosphors can absorb light and then emit it slowly, creating a glow-in-the-dark effect.

- ☐ Instant Ice: Supercooling water allows it to stay liquid below its freezing point. When disturbed, it instantly turns into ice.

- ☐ The Banana Indicator: Bananas contain an enzyme that changes color when exposed to oxygen, turning brown. This is a chemical reaction called oxidation.

- ☐ Non-Newtonian Fluids: Mix cornstarch and water to create a non-Newtonian fluid, which acts like a liquid when moving slowly but solidifies when you apply force.

- ☐ Elephant Toothpaste: A fun chemical reaction involving hydrogen peroxide and yeast creates an explosive foam resembling toothpaste big enough for an elephant.

- ☐ The Smell of Rain: The fresh smell after rain is due to a chemical called geosmin, produced by bacteria in the soil and released into the air.

- ☐ Invisible Ink with Lemon Juice: Writing with lemon juice is invisible until heated, which causes a chemical reaction that turns the writing brown.

- ☐ The Power of Sodium: Sodium reacts vigorously with water, producing heat, hydrogen gas, and sodium hydroxide.

- ☐ Chemical Glow Sticks: Glow sticks produce light through a chemical reaction known as chemiluminescence, where energy is released in the form of light.

- ☐ The Sweetness of Sugar: Sugar molecules bind to sweetness receptors on your tongue, a chemical interaction that sends signals to your brain.

- ☐ Metal Memory: Nitinol, a metal alloy of nickel and titanium, 'remembers' its original shape and returns to it when heated.

- [ ] The Light of Fireflies: Fireflies produce light through a chemical reaction called bioluminescence, which is highly efficient and produces almost no heat.

- [ ] Edible Chemistry: Baking involves numerous chemical reactions, like caramelization and the Maillard reaction, which give baked goods their flavor and color.

- [ ] Liquid Oxygen: Oxygen turns into a pale blue liquid at extremely low temperatures, about -297°F (-183°C).

- [ ] Acid-Base Reactions: Mixing an acid like vinegar with a base like baking soda creates a fizzing reaction, producing carbon dioxide gas.

- [ ] Chemical Garden: By adding metal salts to a silica solution, you can grow colorful, plant-like structures in a chemical garden.

- [ ] Chemiluminescent Luminol: Luminol, used in forensic science, glows blue in the presence of blood due to a chemical reaction called chemiluminescence.

- [ ] Water's Density Anomaly: Water expands when it freezes, which is why ice floats in water – a unique property essential for aquatic life.

Everyday Physics

- [ ] Rainbow Formation: Rainbows are created when sunlight is refracted, or bent, and then reflected inside raindrops, splitting the light into its various colors.

- [ ] Static Electricity and Hair: When you comb your hair and it stands up, it's due to static electricity, which happens when electrons are transferred from your hair to the comb.

- ☐ Boiling Water: When water boils, it undergoes a physical change from a liquid to a gas. This process requires energy, which is why you need to heat water to make it boil.

- ☐ The Science of Bubbles: Soap bubbles demonstrate surface tension. The soap film is made of water sandwiched between two layers of soap molecules, creating a stretchy skin.

- ☐ Magnets and Refrigerators: The reason magnets stick to refrigerators is due to the metal in the fridge door, which gets magnetized by the magnet's field.

- ☐ Shadows on the Wall: Shadows occur when an object blocks light. The size and shape of the shadow depend on the object's shape and the light source's angle.

- ☐ Ice Melting: Ice melts due to heat absorption, causing a phase change from solid to liquid. This is an example of energy transfer.

- ☐ Echoes in a Canyon: An echo happens when sound waves bounce off a distant object and return to the listener, taking longer to return the farther the object is.

- ☐ Condensation on a Cold Glass: Water droplets form on the outside of a cold glass because the cold glass cools the air around it, causing water vapor to condense into liquid.

- ☐ The Moon's Phases: The changing phases of the Moon are caused by the alignment of the Moon, Earth, and Sun, changing how much of the Moon is illuminated and visible from Earth.

- ☐ Sinking and Floating: An object will float if it is less dense than the liquid it is placed in. This principle explains why boats float in water.

- ☐ Mirages on a Road: On hot days, mirages on roads occur due to light bending as it passes through air layers of different temperatures, creating the illusion of water.

- ☐ Sunsets and Sunrises: The beautiful colors of sunsets and sunrises are due to the scattering of sunlight by the Earth's atmosphere, which affects the light's colors.

- ☐ Friction and Heat: Rubbing your hands together quickly generates heat due to friction, the resistance that occurs when two objects move against each other.

- ☐ The Moon's Effect on Tides: Ocean tides are caused primarily by the gravitational pull of the Moon on Earth's oceans.

- ☐ Pressure in a Plane: Airplane cabins are pressurized because the air is thinner at high altitudes, and without pressurization, passengers would have trouble breathing.

- ☐ Why Leaves Change Color: In autumn, leaves change color as the chlorophyll (green pigment) breaks down, revealing other pigments in the leaves.

- ☐ The Doppler Effect: The change in pitch of a siren as an ambulance passes by is due to the Doppler effect, where the sound frequency changes due to the vehicle's motion.

- ☐ Pendulum Motion: A swinging pendulum demonstrates gravitational pull and kinetic energy, showing how potential energy converts to kinetic energy and back.

- ☐ Water's Surface Tension: Water droplets form beads on surfaces due to surface tension, a property of liquid that makes it behave like a stretched elastic sheet.

Fascinating Math Facts

☐ Zero's Origin: The concept of 'zero' as a number was first used in India. It's one of the most important contributions to mathematics, allowing the development of our modern number system.

☐ The Golden Ratio: Appearing in nature, architecture, and art, the Golden Ratio (approximately 1.618) is aesthetically pleasing and has been used in works like the Parthenon and the Mona Lisa.

☐ Infinite Primes: There are infinitely many prime numbers, and mathematicians are still finding larger and larger ones!

☐ Math in Nature: The Fibonacci sequence, where each number is the sum of the two preceding ones, appears in nature in things like the arrangement of leaves on a stem or the pattern of a pineapple's skin.

☐ The Birthday Paradox: In a group of just 23 people, there's a 50% chance that two people will share a birthday. In a group of 70, the probability jumps to 99.9%.

☐ Pi's Infinity: Pi (π), the ratio of a circle's circumference to its diameter, is an infinite decimal and has been calculated to over one trillion digits beyond its decimal point.

☐ Mobius Strip: A surface with only one side and one boundary, the Mobius strip is a fascinating object that challenges our perception of dimensions.

- [ ] The Four Color Theorem: This theorem states that you only need four colors to fill in any map so that no two adjacent regions have the same color.

- [ ] Fractals: Fractals are complex patterns that look similar at any scale and are used to model structures in which similar patterns recur at progressively smaller scales, like snowflakes or coastlines.

- [ ] Kaprekar's Constant: If you take any four-digit number, use its digits to create the largest and smallest numbers possible, and then subtract these numbers, repeating this process, you'll always end up with 6174.

- [ ] Mathematical Beauty: Some mathematicians describe discovering or understanding a particularly elegant mathematical proof as a deeply emotional and aesthetic experience.

- [ ] The Monty Hall Problem: This famous probability puzzle shows that our intuition about probability can often be wrong. It involves three doors, a car, and two goats!

- [ ] Palindromic Numbers: These are numbers that read the same forwards and backwards, like 121 or 12321.

- [ ] Pythagorean Theorem: Known over 2,500 years, it states that in a right-angled triangle, the square of the hypotenuse (the side opposite the right angle) is equal to the sum of the squares of the other two sides.

- [ ] Benford's Law: This law shows that in many naturally occurring collections of numbers, the leading digit is likely to be small. For example, about 30% of the time, a number will start with 1.

- [ ] Non-Euclidean Geometry: This branch of mathematics deals with geometric spaces that are not flat, like the surface of a sphere or a saddle, challenging the traditional rules of geometry.

- [ ] Math and Music: Mathematical patterns underlie the art of music. Ratios and patterns are foundational to musical scales, rhythm, and harmony.

- [ ] The Magic of 9: Multiply any number by 9, then add its digits together and you'll always end up with 9. For example, 9 x 5 = 45, and 4 + 5 = 9.

- [ ] Imaginary Numbers: These are numbers that, when squared, give a negative result. The most famous is the square root of -1, known as 'i.'

- [ ] The Infinite Monkey Theorem: This theorem suggests that a monkey hitting keys at random on a typewriter keyboard for an infinite amount of time will almost surely type any given text, such as the complete works of William Shakespeare.

Amusing Chemicals

- [ ] Laughing Gas: Nitrous oxide, commonly known as laughing gas, can cause uncontrollable laughter when inhaled. It's used in dentistry for its anesthetic and pain-relieving effects.

- [ ] Gallium's Melting Handshake: Gallium is a metal that melts at about 86°F (30°C). If you hold a gallium spoon in your hand, it will melt!

- [ ] Bismuth's Rainbow Staircase: Bismuth, a crystalline metal, forms geometric patterns that look like a futuristic rainbow staircase.

☐ The Smell of Rain: The distinct smell of rain is caused by petrichor, a chemical released from dry soil when it rains.

☐ Dancing Raisins: In a glass of soda, raisins can "dance" up and down due to carbon dioxide bubbles attaching and detaching from their wrinkled surface.

☐ Glow-in-the-Dark Radium: In the early 20th century, radium was used to make watch dials glow in the dark, before its radioactive hazards were known.

☐ Banana Radiation: Bananas are slightly radioactive due to the potassium they contain. Don't worry, you'd need to eat millions at once for any effect!

☐ Mercury's Mood Swings: Mercury is the only metal that is liquid at room temperature. Its temperature sensitivity makes it perfect for thermometers.

☐ Hot Ice: Sodium acetate trihydrate, a chemical in reusable heat packs, crystallizes instantly from liquid to solid, releasing heat and creating "hot ice."

☐ Oobleck, The Non-Newtonian Fluid: A mixture of cornstarch and water, named after a Dr. Seuss story, behaves as a solid under pressure and a liquid at rest.

☐ Caffeine Crystal Beauty: Under a microscope, caffeine forms beautiful, needle-like crystals.

☐ Burning Ice: Methane hydrate looks like ice but burns when lit, as it's methane gas trapped in water crystals.

☐ The Forbidden Fruit Flavor: Ethyl formate, found in raspberries, is also present in space, giving some cosmic dust clouds a raspberry-like scent and taste.

☐ Color-Changing Alexandrite Effect: Some chemicals can change color based on the light source, much like the rare gemstone alexandrite.

☐ The Chameleon Metal: Titanium can be anodized to various colors without any pigments, just by changing the thickness of its oxide layer.

☐ Copper's Colorful Corrosion: When copper corrodes, it forms a blue-green patina known as verdigris, seen on roofs and statues like the Statue of Liberty.

☐ Dry Water: This powder form of water contains tiny droplets of liquid water surrounded by a sandy silica coating.

☐ Vantablack: This substance is one of the darkest artificial substances known, absorbing up to 99.965% of visible light.

☐ Ferrofluid Fun: Ferrofluids are liquids that become strongly magnetized in the presence of a magnetic field, forming spiky, alien-like shapes.

☐ NeverWet Surfaces: Hydrophobic coatings can repel water so effectively that liquids roll off without wetting the surface, like water droplets on a lotus leaf.

Unusual Musical Records

☐ The Longest Piano Performance: In 2009, Romuald Koperski played piano for 103 hours straight in Poland, setting a world record.

☐ The World's Largest Guitar: In 2000, a 43-foot-long guitar was built in the United States, modeled after a Gibson Flying V.

- ☐ The Oldest Musical Composition: The oldest known melody, the "Hurrian Hymn," dates back to 1400 BC and was discovered in Ugarit, now part of Syria.

- ☐ Most Languages in One Song: The song "Let the World Be Ours Tonight" by Deborah Cox has been recorded in 42 different languages.

- ☐ The Highest Vocal Note by a Male: Adam Lopez holds this record, hitting a note in the stratosphere, specifically a C8, which is as high as the keys on a piano go.

- ☐ The Fastest Violin Player: In 2010, Ben Lee played "Flight of the Bumblebee" at 15 notes per second, setting a world record.

- ☐ The Largest Orchestra: In 2016, a record was set in Germany with an orchestra of 7,548 musicians.

- ☐ The Longest Marathon Singing by a Child: Suchetha Satish, a 12-year-old girl from India, sang for over 120 songs in 102 languages in a marathon session lasting over 6 hours.

- ☐ The Most Concerts in 24 Hours: Hunter Hayes performed 10 concerts across 10 cities within 24 hours in 2014, breaking the previous record.

- ☐ The Oldest Professional Orchestra: The Royal Danish Orchestra, founded in 1448, is the oldest continuously operating orchestra.

- ☐ Most Simultaneous Singing Performances: Over 300,000 people in China sang the song "My Chinese Heart" simultaneously in different locations in 2004.

☐ The Longest Echo in a Man-Made Structure: The echo inside the Inchindown oil storage tanks in Scotland lasts for 75 seconds.

☐ The World's Smallest Violin: Measuring just 1.27 cm in length, the world's smallest playable violin was created by Chen Lianzhi in 2010.

☐ The Largest Harmonica Ensemble: In 2009, 6,131 participants in Hong Kong played "Do-Re-Mi" on the harmonica together.

☐ The Longest Guitar Solo: In 2011, David DiDonato played a guitar solo for 24 hours and 55 minutes in the United States.

☐ Most Different Musical Instruments Played in One Concert: Neil Nayyar in the USA played 107 different instruments in a single concert in 2018.

☐ The First Music Video in Space: Canadian astronaut Chris Hadfield recorded the first music video in space, a cover of David Bowie's "Space Oddity" aboard the International Space Station.

☐ The Deepest Underground Concert: A Finnish band called Agonizer played a concert 1,400 meters underground in the Pyhäsalmi Mine in 2007.

☐ The Most People Playing the Same Piano: In 2013, 21 musicians in China played the same piano simultaneously.

☐ The Longest Handbell Marathon: In 2010, two teams in the United Kingdom played the handbells for a record 24 hours, covering 512 different pieces of music.

Funny Musical Experiments

☐ In 1957, scientists at the University of Cambridge conducted an experiment where the sound of a cannon was used to create music. This project was known as "Music from Cannons."

☐ In 2013, a group of musicians performed a concert using only instruments made from vegetables. They played on carrots, broccoli, and pumpkins.

☐ In 1969, an architect from the United States built a house that played music when rain fell on its roof. This musical house was called the "Rain House."

☐ A group of researchers in Switzerland created music using only sounds produced by their bodies and clothing. Their performances are called "musical telescopes."

☐ In 2010, an album was released that was recorded solely using sounds made by animals. The project involved sounds of birds, frogs, and other animals.

☐ A group of Japanese researchers conducted an experiment where they created music using only the sounds produced by falling water droplets.

☐ In 2008, a bridge that played music when cars drove across it was constructed by an architect in the UK. This bridge was named the "Musical Bridge."

☐ There is an instrument in Alaska called the "Iceophone," which is made from ice blocks, and it is played using bones.

☐ In the 1980s, Atari released a video game called "The Home Game," in which players could create music by interacting within a virtual home.

☐ A group of musicians from France created music using the sounds produced by various types of cheese. This project is known as the "Cheese Symphony."

☐ In 2007, an album was released where all tracks were recorded using instruments made from old toys.

☐ In the 1960s, researchers created music using only sounds generated by computers. This style of music was called "computer music."

☐ In 1994, a group of musicians performed a concert using instruments made from old car parts.

☐ In 2009, researchers in Germany conducted an experiment where they created music using only sounds produced by various types of plastic.

☐ In the 1970s, Moog created a synthesizer that allowed musicians to play the instrument using eye movements.

☐ A group of Canadian researchers conducted an experiment in which they created music using only sounds produced by various bird species.

☐ In the 1980s, a program was developed that allowed people to create music using the sounds produced by computer printers.

☐ In 2012, a group of musicians created music using sounds produced by medical devices such as stethoscopes and electrocardiograms.

- [ ] In Japan, there is a tradition of creating music using the sounds produced by koto-fones, musical instruments made from wood and leather.

- [ ] In the 1960s, a "Random Music Generator" was created, which generated music entirely randomly, without the involvement of musicians.

Musical Instruments

- [ ] Oldest Musical Instrument: The world's oldest known musical instrument is a bone flute that dates back 40,000 years.

- [ ] Longest Guitar: The longest guitar ever recorded in the Guinness World Records measures over 13 meters in length.

- [ ] Heaviest Guitar: The heaviest guitar in the world weighs approximately 140 kilograms and was created in Canada.

- [ ] Smallest Violin: The world's smallest violin measures just 16 centimeters in length and was crafted in 1985.

- [ ] Deep Bass: The lowest playable note on a double bass is called "C-subcontra" and is so deep that it's inaudible to the human ear but can be felt as vibrations.

- [ ] Amphora Guitar: A musician in Greece created a guitar from an ancient amphora, giving it a unique sound.

- [ ] Glass Harmonicas: In the 18th century, glass harmonicas were popular, and they were played by wetting one's fingers and sliding them along glass bowls to create hauntingly beautiful sounds.

- [ ] Ancient Duduk: The duduk, an ancient Armenian instrument, is considered one of the oldest wooden wind instruments.

- [ ] Electronic Sampling: Many modern songs are created by sampling sounds and melodies from other songs, making them electronically unique.

- [ ] Water-Based Music: Musicians in Japan experimented with creating music using sounds produced by falling water droplets.

- [ ] The Glass Bridge: In 2008, a bridge in the UK, known as the "Musical Bridge," played music as cars passed over it.

- [ ] Iceophone: In Alaska, there's an instrument called the "Iceophone," made from ice blocks and played with bones.

- [ ] Electronic Music: In the 1960s, researchers created music solely using sounds generated by computers, pioneering the genre of "computer music."

- [ ] Toy Instruments: In 2007, an album was released featuring tracks recorded using instruments made from old toys.

- [ ] Medical Devices in Music: In 2012, musicians created music using sounds produced by medical instruments such as stethoscopes and electrocardiograms.

- [ ] Koto-Fones: In Japan, musicians create music using sounds produced by "koto-fones," instruments made from wood and leather.

☐ Random Music Generator: In the 1960s, a "Random Music Generator" was created, generating music entirely randomly without human intervention.

☐ Piano in Space: Pianos were sent into space for astronauts to play, creating music in zero gravity.

☐ Most Expensive Violin: The most expensive violin in the world is a Stradivarius sold for $16 million.

☐ Ancient Organ: The world's oldest functioning organ, dating back to 1435, is located in Bavaria, Germany.

Music Historical Moments

☐ Birth of Opera: The world's first opera, "Dafne," was composed by Jacopo Peri in 1597 in Italy, marking the birth of the opera genre.

☐ Stratospheric Voice: Renowned soprano Maria Callas possessed a vocal range spanning over three octaves, making it one of the widest in opera history.

☐ Paganini's Virtuosity: Virtuoso violinist Niccolò Paganini was accused of collaborating with the devil due to his extraordinary technical abilities.

☐ Symphony of Cannons: In 1812, during the French invasion of Moscow, Pyotr Ilyich Tchaikovsky composed his famous "1812 Overture," incorporating actual cannon fire.

☐ Beethoven's Deafness: Ludwig van Beethoven continued to compose music even when he became deaf, with his Ninth Symphony being created when he could no longer hear.

☐ Jazz Improvisation: Jazz musicians often use improvisation, creating music on the spot, making each performance unique.

☐ Rock Revolution: In 1954, Bill Haley's song "Rock Around the Clock" became a symbol of rock 'n' roll and triggered the rock revolution.

☐ The Fab Four: The Beatles were the first band to hold all top five positions on the American Billboard Hot 100 simultaneously with five different singles.

☐ Rock Ballad: Queen's "Bohemian Rhapsody" is one of the most complex and lengthy rock ballads in history and became a chart-topping hit.

☐ Beethoven's Ninth: Beethoven began work on his "Ninth Symphony" before having a clear vision of its form, creating a masterpiece of Western classical music.

☐ Vikings and Music: Vikings used music and melodies to convey and preserve their history and culture.

☐ Stradivarius Violins: Violins crafted by Antonio Stradivari in the 17th century are considered the finest in the world, with some valued in the millions.

☐ Ladies' Orchestra: In the early 20th century, Australia had an all-female orchestra, one of the world's first composed entirely of women.

☐ Ancient Chinese Music: Ancient China produced some of the world's earliest musical instruments, such as the guqin and dizi, still used today.

☐ Musical "Moonwalk": The first moonwalk by a human was accompanied by music, as astronauts played the tin whistle on the Moon.

- [ ] The Theremin: The theremin is one of the most unusual musical instruments, played without physical contact, by manipulating sound with hand movements in the air.

- [ ] NBA Theme: The NBA's iconic theme, heard before every game, was based on music composed by Jerry Goldsmith.

- [ ] Musical Notation: Modern musical notation, used today, has roots dating back over 1000 years BCE.

- [ ] Composer Focus: Modest Mussorgsky composed the opera "Boris Godunov" at the request of famed opera singer Fyodor Chaliapin.

- [ ] Rock 'n' Roll on the Moon: The crew of Apollo 17 played "Rock and Roll" on the Moon during their mission in 1972.

Funny Film Techniques

- [ ] Animatronics: To create realistic monsters and creatures in movies, animatronics are used – robotic models operated by puppeteers.

- [ ] Sound Effects: Sound effects are often created in unconventional ways; for instance, the sound of clanking armor might involve a pizza being tossed.

- [ ] Green Screen: A green screen is used to add background images or videos in post-production, giving the illusion that the action is taking place in different locations.

- [ ] Stunt Doubles: Not all actors perform dangerous stunts themselves; special stunt doubles take on risky scenes.

- ☐ Wire Work: Many flying scenes in films are achieved through the use of wires and specialized harnesses.

- ☐ Mechanical Costumes: To create robots and superheroes, costumes with built-in mechanisms for movement are often used.

- ☐ Slow-Motion: The slow-motion effect is achieved by shooting at high speeds and then playing the footage back at a reduced speed.

- ☐ Miniatures: Miniature models of cities and explosions are created for filming destruction scenes.

- ☐ Headless Actors: For scenes where a character loses their head, special mannequins and effects are used.

- ☐ Fire Stunts: Flame effects in films are often created using pyrotechnics and fire-resistant costumes.

- ☐ Wire Dancing: In musicals and fantasy films, actors may dance while suspended on wires for a weightless effect.

- ☐ Artificial Rain: To create rain on set, watering systems and artificial raindrops are used.

- ☐ Masks for Actors: In sci-fi movies, actors may wear masks to appear as aliens or monsters.

- ☐ Telephoto Lenses: Telescopic lenses allow for smooth zooming in and out, creating dramatic shots.

- ☐ Ice Sculptures: Large ice sculptures are crafted for scenes set in icy landscapes.

- [ ] Playing with Shadows: Lighting and shadow effects are often used to create intrigue and atmosphere.

- [ ] Mini Cameras: Miniature cameras can be mounted almost anywhere for unique angles.

- [ ] Fake Blood: For scenes with injuries or battles, artificial blood is created using various recipes.

- [ ] Cinematic Innovations: Inventors constantly develop new techniques and tricks to make movies more thrilling.

- [ ] Art of Editing: Film editing is the art of assembling all scenes and effects to create a cinematic masterpiece.

Cult Films

- [ ] "Star Wars": This franchise became a massive phenomenon, inspiring numerous space and adventure films.

- [ ] "The Lord of the Rings": The films set in Middle-earth have become classics in the fantasy genre, influencing many other works.

- [ ] "The Matrix": This film revolutionized the science fiction genre and inspired countless imitations and parodies.

- [ ] "Harry Potter": The saga of the young wizard became a cultural touchstone, influencing literature and cinema worldwide.

- [ ] "A Clockwork Orange": This film sparked controversy and had a profound impact on both cinema and culture.

- [ ] "The Terminator": This film introduced the concept of cyborgs and artificial intelligence, influencing many other movies.

- [ ] "Toy Story": Pixar's first fully computer-animated film changed the world of animation.

- [ ] "2001: A Space Odyssey": Stanley Kubrick's film redefined science fiction and visual effects.

- [ ] "The Truman Show": This film sparked discussions about privacy and reality.

- [ ] "Eternal Sunshine of the Spotless Mind": The film explores the complexities of human relationships and memory.

- [ ] "Only Old Men Are Going to Battle": This Soviet film became a cult classic in Russia and inspired many directors.

- [ ] "The Godfather": This film inspired countless other crime dramas and series.

- [ ] "The Shawshank Redemption": This film about hope and friendship is one of the most beloved in cinematic history.

- [ ] "Blade Runner": The film introduced the cyberpunk genre and had a major impact on science fiction.

- [ ] "Home Alone": This film about a young boy's adventures inspired many comedies.

- [ ] "Reservoir Dogs": Quentin Tarantino's film had a significant impact on the style and rhythm of cinema.

- [ ] "Operation Y and Other Shurik's Adventures": This Soviet comedy became a cult classic and influenced many comedians.

- [ ] "Mr. Bean": The character of Mr. Bean became internationally famous and inspired comedic actors.

- [ ] "Jurassic Park": The film about resurrected dinosaurs made movie effects more realistic.

- [ ] "Titanic": This film became one of the most successful in history and influenced the romantic drama genre.

Special Effects in Cinema

- [ ] Early Special Effects: The earliest special effects in movies were created using mirrors and simple optical illusions.

- [ ] Stop-Motion Animation: Stop-motion animation allowed for bringing inanimate objects to life, creating magical effects.

- [ ] Black Screens: Black screens were used to create the invisibility effect, allowing actors to interact with invisible objects.

- [ ] Miniatures: Miniature models were created for shooting city destruction and explosions.

- [ ] Advancements in CGI: With the development of computer-generated imagery (CGI), realistic visual effects became possible.

- [ ] Motion Capture: Motion capture technology allowed for capturing actors' movements and transferring them to computer-generated characters.

☐ Green Screen: The green screen became the standard for creating background images and visual effects.

☐ Life-Sized Costumes: Life-sized costumes were used to create realistic monsters and creatures.

☐ Artistic Filters: Camera lens filters were used to create various effects, including soft focus and sepia tones.

☐ Fire and Water Effects: Artificial flames and water effects became safer and more realistic.

☐ Animatronics: Robotic puppets and models were used for lifelike movements and expressions.

☐ Slow-Motion Effects: Slow-motion effects were achieved by shooting at high speeds and playing back at reduced speeds.

☐ Optical Illusions: Mirrors and glass were used to create teleportation and cloning effects.

☐ Practical Prosthetics: The use of practical prosthetics and makeup helped actors transform into different characters.

☐ Wirework: Special wires and harnesses enabled actors to perform gravity-defying stunts.

☐ Artificial Blood: Various artificial blood recipes were created for scenes with injuries and battles.

☐ Underwater Filming: Waterproof cameras and equipment allowed for underwater shooting.

☐ Animatronic Animals: Animatronic animals were used for realistic animal behavior in movies.

☐ Mixed Special Effects: Modern films often combine various special effects techniques for maximum realism.

☐ Virtual Reality: VR technologies open up new possibilities for creating stunning visual effects and interactive movie experiences.

Film's Remarkable Records

☐ Most Anticipated Film: James Cameron's "Avatar" was in development and production for over 10 years.

☐ Most Expensive Film: "Avatar" also holds the record for the most expensive film, with a budget of over $2.5 billion.

☐ Highest-Paid Actor: Robert Downey Jr. received a record-breaking paycheck of $75 million for his role in "The Avengers."

☐ Highest-Grossing Film: "Avatar" held the title of the highest-grossing film in history for a long time.

☐ Longest Acting Career: Kirk Douglas appeared in a film at the age of 101.

☐ Youngest Oscar Winner: Tatum O'Neal won an Oscar at the age of 10.

☐ Most On-Screen Villain Deaths in One Film: "Lethal Weapon 3" features over 200 slain villains.

☐ Longest Filming Time: "Fight Club" took 138 days to shoot, considered a lengthy period for a drama.

☐ Most Visual Effects: "Pirates of the Caribbean: At World's End" boasts over 2,000 visual effects shots.

☐ Largest Movie Studio: Ireland's "Ashford Studios" is the largest film studio in the world.

☐ Longest Time to Create a Movie Mask: Crafting the Alien mask in "Alien" took over 3 months.

☐ Most Makeup Used on an Actor: "The Lord of the Rings: The Return of the King" used 1,200 liters of makeup.

☐ Most Stunt Performers in One Scene: "Ben-Hur" featured 8,000 stunt performers in an epic battle.

☐ Highest Pay Per Minute in a Film: Matthew McConaughey earned $207,000 per minute for "The Wolf of Wall Street."

☐ Most Sequels Simultaneously Filmed: The "Fast & Furious" franchise has produced 9 sequels (as of 2022).

☐ Most Academy Awards for a Film: "Ben-Hur" and "Titanic" each won 11 Oscars.

☐ Longest Fight Scene in Film: The fight in "Enter the Dragon" lasted approximately 11 minutes.

☐ Longest Dubbing in Film History: Actor Martin Sheen holds the record for voicing a character in an animated film for over 15 years.

- [ ] Longest Film: "Gandhi" has a runtime of 191 minutes (over 3 hours).

- [ ] Most Parallel Camera Setups: "The Matrix Reloaded" employed 35 parallel cameras to shoot a scene.

Olympic Games History

- [ ] Sacred Ground: The Olympic Games took place in Ancient Greece on sacred land in Olympia.

- [ ] Inception of the Games: The first Olympic Games were held in 776 BCE and featured only foot racing.

- [ ] Single Event: Initially, there was only one event - a 192-meter foot race.

- [ ] Naked Sport: All participants competed naked in the early Olympic Games.

- [ ] The Word "Olympic": The word "Olympic" is derived from "Olympia," referring to its connection with the Olympic Games.

- [ ] Ancient Heroes: The Olympic Games were dedicated to Greek gods like Zeus and Hercules.

- [ ] Duration of the Games: The Olympics lasted for 5 days and included not only competitions but also religious ceremonies.

- [ ] Golden Laurels: Winners in Ancient Greece received olive wreaths rather than gold medals.

- [ ] First Female Victory: The first female victor was Kyniska, who won in "horse racing" (an unusual event combining racing and running).

- [ ] Disappearance of the Games: Olympic Games were banned in 393 CE by the Roman Empire.

- [ ] Revival: The Olympic Games were revived in 1896 in Athens.

- [ ] National Flags: The tradition of raising the flags of participating nations began at the 1908 Olympics.

- [ ] Winter Olympics: The Winter Olympics were first held in 1924 in France.

- [ ] Collectible Pins: Collecting Olympic pins featuring event logos became popular in the early 20th century.

- [ ] Olympic Flag: The Olympic flag with five rings symbolizing the continents was introduced in 1913.

- [ ] Guest Cities: Olympic Games are hosted by different cities every four years.

- [ ] Gold from Silver: Silver medals, awarded to runners-up, are actually coated with a thin layer of gold.

- [ ] Sportsmanship: The Olympic spirit emphasizes competition for victory but within the bounds of fair play.

- [ ] Olympic Torch: The tradition of the Olympic flame and torch began in 1936 at the Berlin Olympics.

- [ ] Sporting Legacy: The Olympic Games continue to inspire athletes and promote global unity.

Olympic Oddities

- [ ] Race Walking: Race walking is an Olympic sport where participants must maintain contact with the ground at all times, and one foot must be on the ground at all times. It's like speed walking with strict rules.

- [ ] Trampoline Gymnastics: Trampoline gymnastics involves athletes performing acrobatic moves on a trampoline, bouncing high in the air while executing flips and twists.

- [ ] Modern Pentathlon: The modern pentathlon combines five diverse sports: fencing, swimming, equestrian show jumping, pistol shooting, and cross-country running. It originated from the skills required by a 19th-century cavalry soldier.

- [ ] Biathlon: The biathlon combines cross-country skiing and rifle shooting. Athletes must ski for a certain distance and then stop to shoot at targets. It requires both physical endurance and precision.

- [ ] Table Tennis: Table tennis, or ping pong, may seem ordinary, but it's an Olympic sport that demands incredible speed, reflexes, and precision.

- [ ] Curling: Curling is often referred to as "chess on ice." Players slide stones on a sheet of ice towards a target area while team members use brooms to control the stone's direction.

- [ ] Skeleton: Skeleton is a winter sport where athletes lie face down on a small sled and navigate a twisting, frozen track at high speeds. It's a thrilling and dangerous event.

- ☐ Tug of War: Tug of war was an Olympic sport from 1900 to 1920. Teams competed to pull a rope in their direction, trying to move a marker on the ground.

- ☐ Live Pigeon Shooting: In the early 20th century, live pigeon shooting was an Olympic event where participants aimed to shoot as many pigeons as possible. Thankfully, this sport was discontinued.

- ☐ Solo Synchronized Swimming: While synchronized swimming is typically a team sport, solo synchronized swimming is a mesmerizing event where a single athlete performs synchronized routines in the water.

- ☐ Pistol Dueling: Pistol dueling was an event in the 1906 Olympics where participants shot at mannequins dressed as dummies. It was a short-lived and odd sport.

- ☐ Rhythmic Gymnastics: Rhythmic gymnastics combines ballet, dance, and gymnastics with props like ribbons, hoops, and balls. Athletes perform graceful routines while manipulating these objects.

- ☐ Rope Climbing: Rope climbing was an Olympic event in the early 20th century. Competitors climbed up a hanging rope without using their legs.

- ☐ Roller Hockey: Roller hockey, a variation of ice hockey, was included in the 1992 Olympics as a demonstration sport.

- ☐ Underwater Swimming: Underwater swimming was part of the 1900 Olympics. Athletes swam underwater for as long as they could, which is no longer part of the modern Olympic program.

- ☐ Plunge for Distance: The plunge for distance was a unique swimming event where athletes dove into the water and glided underwater for as long as possible.

- ☐ Military Patrol: Military patrol was a precursor to modern biathlon, combining cross-country skiing, rifle shooting, and military tactics.

- ☐ Poodle Clipping: Poodle clipping was part of the 1900 Olympics, where athletes demonstrated their skills in grooming and styling poodles.

- ☐ Firefighting: Firefighting was an event in the 1900 Olympics. Teams competed in a race to extinguish a fire and save a victim using period firefighting equipment.

Olympic Laughs

- ☐ Underwater Escape: In the 1900 Paris Olympics, a French swimmer, Charles Devendeville, swam to freedom during the 200-meter obstacle swim event when he noticed the water was too dirty.

- ☐ Marathon Prank: During the 1904 St. Louis Olympics, the marathon saw bizarre incidents like runners getting lost, one athlete hitching a car ride, and another ingesting strychnine but surviving.

- ☐ Solo Sailing: At the 1988 Seoul Olympics, a Bulgarian sailor, Tereza Marinova, won a gold medal in the women's sailing event because she was the only competitor.

- ☐ Punching in Synchronized Swimming: In the 2012 London Olympics, a camera operator accidentally punched a synchronized swimmer during a performance.

☐ False Start Fright: In the 2000 Sydney Olympics, a swimmer was so startled by a false start that he leaped out of the pool, thinking he had already finished his race.

☐ Naked Intruder: During the men's marathon at the 2004 Athens Olympics, a man wearing nothing but a tanga brief ran onto the course before being apprehended.

☐ Flag Switch: In the 1936 Berlin Olympics, a Japanese pole vaulter, Shuhei Nishida, and a German jumper, Hans Lutz, tied for second place. They swapped flags, and both countries are credited with the silver medal.

☐ Cocktail Celebration: After winning the gold medal in 2008, Jamaican sprinter Usain Bolt celebrated by drinking a cocktail on the track in Beijing.

☐ Animal Intrusion: In the 1964 Tokyo Olympics, a stray dog ran onto the track during the men's marathon and even outran some of the runners.

☐ Empty Victory Stand: In the 1900 Paris Olympics, many athletes didn't show up for the award ceremonies, so local children were recruited to stand in as medalists.

☐ Mismatched Shoes: Czechoslovakian tennis player Miloslav Mecir wore mismatched shoes at the 1988 Seoul Olympics because he couldn't find a matching pair.

☐ Shoeless Joe: Ethiopian runner Abebe Bikila won the 1960 Rome Marathon while running barefoot because his shoes gave him blisters.

☐ Wrong Medal Ceremony: In the 2008 Beijing Olympics, an official mistakenly presented the wrong medal during the women's high jump ceremony.

☐ Wardrobe Malfunction: During the 2004 Athens Olympics, Greek weightlifter Pyrros Dimas tore his shorts while attempting a lift but continued his performance unfazed.

☐ Invisible Sailors: In the 1972 Munich Olympics, the sailing competition was canceled for several days due to lack of wind, leaving sailors with nothing to do.

☐ Dropped Torch: During the 1956 Melbourne Olympics, the torchbearer stumbled and dropped the Olympic torch, but it was quickly relit.

☐ Last-Minute Entry: Swimmer Eric "the Eel" Moussambani from Equatorial Guinea, who had only trained in a hotel pool, competed in the 100m freestyle at the 2000 Sydney Olympics.

☐ Runaway Canoe: In the 2000 Sydney Olympics, a German canoeist's boat capsized, and he had to chase it down the course to finish the race.

☐ Empty Pool: During the 1988 Seoul Olympics, a sudden rainstorm filled the diving pool with so much water that it had to be emptied and refilled.

☐ Costume Mix-Up: The Chinese diving team accidentally wore their practice suits instead of competition suits during the 2012 London Olympics.

Sporting Achievements

- [ ] The 100-Point Game: In 1962, NBA legend Wilt Chamberlain scored an astonishing 100 points in a single basketball game.

- [ ] Unbeaten Streak: Boxer Rocky Marciano retired undefeated with a record of 49-0, a feat unmatched in heavyweight boxing.

- [ ] The Perfect Ten: Romanian gymnast Nadia Comăneci achieved the first-ever perfect 10.0 score in gymnastics at the 1976 Olympics.

- [ ] Four-Minute Mile: British runner Roger Bannister became the first person to run a mile in under four minutes in 1954.

- [ ] Grand Slam in a Single Inning: Fernando Tatis hit two grand slams in one inning during a baseball game in 1999, an unparalleled feat.

- [ ] Fastest 100 Meters: Usain Bolt holds the world record for the fastest 100 meters, completing it in just 9.58 seconds.

- [ ] The Double Triple-Double: In 1961-62, NBA star Oscar Robertson averaged a triple-double for the entire season, a feat not matched for over 55 years.

- [ ] The Iron Man: Cal Ripken Jr. played in 2,632 consecutive baseball games, breaking Lou Gehrig's record.

- [ ] Most Goals in a Year: Footballer Lionel Messi scored a record-breaking 91 goals in 2012, surpassing Gerd Muller's previous record.

- ☐ The Perfect Game: In 1956, Don Larsen pitched a perfect game in the World Series, retiring every batter without a single one reaching base.

- ☐ The Highest Basketball Shot: Thunder Law made a basket from a record-breaking 34.29 meters (112 feet 6 inches) in 2016.

- ☐ The Fastest Serve: Tennis player Samuel Groth hit the fastest serve ever recorded at 263.4 km/h (163.7 mph) in 2012.

- ☐ The Oldest Olympian: Oscar Swahn, a Swedish shooter, competed in the 1920 Olympics at the age of 72.

- ☐ Youngest Olympic Gymnast: Dimitrios Loundras from Greece participated in the 1896 Athens Olympics at the age of 10.

- ☐ Six Consecutive NBA Titles: Bill Russell led the Boston Celtics to six consecutive NBA championships from 1957 to 1962.

- ☐ Most Consecutive Wins: Tennis player Martina Navratilova won 74 consecutive matches in 1984.

- ☐ The Longest Tennis Match: John Isner and Nicolas Mahut played the longest tennis match in history, lasting 11 hours and 5 minutes over three days.

- ☐ Most Olympic Golds: Swimmer Michael Phelps holds the record for the most Olympic gold medals, with 23.

- ☐ The Triple-Double Machine: NBA player Russell Westbrook holds the record for the most career triple-doubles.

☐ Four Home Runs in a Game: Baseball legend Babe Ruth achieved the rare feat of hitting four home runs in a single game in 1922.

Extreme Sports

☐ Base Jumping Records: Base jumping from the world's tallest building, the Burj Khalifa, is an extreme feat accomplished by daring individuals.

☐ Biggest Waves Surfed: Surfers like Garrett McNamara have ridden some of the biggest waves, including a record-breaking 101-foot wave in Portugal.

☐ Skydiving from the Edge of Space: Felix Baumgartner set records by skydiving from a height of 128,100 feet, breaking the sound barrier during his descent.

☐ Wingsuit Flying: Wingsuit flyers glide through the air at speeds of up to 150 mph, maneuvering through narrow gaps in cliffs and mountains.

☐ Free Solo Climbing: Alex Honnold's free solo ascent of El Capitan in Yosemite National Park amazed the world with its sheer audacity.

☐ Ice Climbing Waterfalls: Ice climbers scale frozen waterfalls in places like Norway, challenging both their strength and the cold.

☐ Downhill Mountain Biking: Extreme downhill bikers navigate steep, rocky, and treacherous terrains at incredible speeds.

☐ Highlining Over Canyons: Slackliners walk on thin lines suspended high above canyons, often without safety nets.

☐ Volcano Boarding: Adventurers slide down active volcanoes on specially designed boards, like Cerro Negro in Nicaragua.

☐ Cliff Diving: Cliff divers leap from dizzying heights into bodies of water, executing breathtaking aerial maneuvers.

☐ Freestyle Motocross: FMX riders perform gravity-defying tricks on their motorcycles, soaring through the air.

☐ Parkour and Freerunning: Traceurs and freerunners leap, vault, and flip over urban obstacles with incredible agility.

☐ Snowkiting: Snowkiters use the power of the wind to glide across snowy landscapes on skis or snowboards.

☐ White Water Kayaking: Extreme kayakers brave treacherous rapids and waterfalls, navigating dangerous whitewater.

☐ Cave Diving: Cave divers explore underwater cave systems, often in complete darkness, with specialized equipment.

☐ Sandboarding: Sandboarders ride down enormous sand dunes in desert regions, like the dunes of Namibia.

☐ Volcano Surfing: Some thrill-seekers slide down the slopes of active volcanoes on specially designed boards.

☐ High Altitude Mountaineering: Climbers face extreme cold, altitude sickness, and avalanches while scaling the world's tallest peaks.

☐ Street Luge: Street luge involves racing downhill on a small, low-slung board at speeds exceeding 60 mph.

☐ Underwater Ice Hockey: Players don diving gear and use special sticks to play ice hockey beneath the frozen surface of a lake.

Funny Sports Traditions

☐ The Curse of the Billy Goat: The Chicago Cubs were supposedly cursed in 1945 when a fan and his pet goat were ejected from Wrigley Field, leading to a 71-year World Series drought.

☐ Soccer Players and Haircuts: Many soccer players believe their performance is linked to their hairstyle, leading to pre-game haircuts for good luck.

☐ Hockey's Playoff Beards: It's a tradition in ice hockey for players to stop shaving during the playoffs, believing it brings good luck to their team.

☐ Kissing the Yard of Bricks: Winners of the Indianapolis 500 car race traditionally kiss the yard of bricks at the finish line, a practice that started in 1996.

☐ Rally Caps in Baseball: When a team needs to make a comeback, players and fans turn their caps inside out or backwards as a sign of support and luck.

☐ The All Blacks' Haka: Before rugby matches, New Zealand's All Blacks perform a traditional Maori haka dance to intimidate the opposition and honor their heritage.

☐ The Gatorade Shower: It's a common American football tradition to douse the winning coach with a cooler of Gatorade at the end of a significant game.

☐ Tennis Players Bouncing the Ball: Many tennis players bounce the ball a specific number of times before serving, believing it improves their focus and luck.

☐ Cricket's Red Underwear: Some cricket players wear red underwear during games for good luck, a tradition with roots in superstition.

☐ Golfers' Lucky Charms: Many golfers carry lucky charms, like special coins or markers, believing they improve their game.

☐ Synchronized Swimmers' Gelatin: Synchronized swimmers often use gelatin to keep their hair in place underwater, a quirky yet practical tradition.

☐ Baseball's Seventh-Inning Stretch: During the seventh inning of a baseball game, fans stand and stretch, a tradition believed to have been started by President William Howard Taft.

☐ Boxers Skipping Sex Before Matches: Many boxers adhere to the superstition of abstaining from sex before a fight, believing it enhances their strength and focus.

☐ Soccer's Pre-Game Tunnel Ritual: Before a soccer match, players often have specific routines in the tunnel like jumping, handshakes, or even tying and retying their shoelaces.

☐ Lucky Socks in Sports: Athletes in various sports wear 'lucky socks' during important games, often unwashed to preserve the luck.

- [ ] Basketball's Free-Throw Rituals: Basketball players have unique routines before free throws, including specific dribbles and gestures, for consistency and luck.

- [ ] Spitting in Baseball: Players spit on their hands or gloves for better grip, a longstanding baseball tradition.

- [ ] The Stanley Cup Superstitions: In hockey, it's considered bad luck to touch the Stanley Cup if you haven't won it.

- [ ] Marathoners' Pasta Dinners: Before a race, many marathon runners eat a pasta dinner for carb-loading, believing it boosts their energy reserves.

- [ ] Olympic Village Superstitions: Some Olympians bring items like photos, stuffed animals, or special pillows to the Olympic Village for good luck and a sense of home.

Sports Myths

- [ ] Basketball Hoops are 10 Feet High Everywhere: The standard basketball hoop height of 10 feet was established over a century ago and has never changed, leading to the myth that all players have adapted to this height universally.

- [ ] The Curse of the Bambino: A famous baseball myth suggests that the Boston Red Sox were cursed after trading Babe Ruth, aka "The Bambino," to the New York Yankees, leading to an 86-year championship drought.

- [ ] Soccer and War: A widespread myth is that a soccer game between Honduras and El Salvador ignited a war in 1969. While tensions were high due to the match, the causes of the war were more complex.

- [ ] 5-Minute Rule in Tennis: Some believe that tennis matches cannot end within five minutes of the hour. However, this is just a myth, as matches can conclude at any time.

- [ ] The Rally Cap Magic: In baseball, the myth of the rally cap suggests that turning your cap inside out can magically help your team stage a comeback.

- [ ] The No-White-After-Labor-Day Rule in Tennis: This myth dictates that players should avoid white tennis outfits after Labor Day, but it's merely a fashion guideline, not a rule.

- [ ] Golf's 18-Hole Standard: A popular myth suggests that there are 18 holes in golf because there are 18 shots in a bottle of whiskey, one for each hole.

- [ ] The Madden Curse: A myth in American football where players who appear on the cover of the Madden NFL video game are believed to suffer bad luck, injuries, or poor performance.

- [ ] Double Dribble Misconceptions: Some believe double dribbling in basketball involves dribbling with both hands. It actually refers to stopping and restarting dribbling or dribbling with both hands.

- [ ] The Five-Second Rule in Basketball: Contrary to popular belief, the five-second rule doesn't apply once a player starts dribbling.

- [ ] Cricket's Tea Break Tradition: There's a myth that cricket's tea breaks were introduced for strategic discussions. They were actually just for refreshment and rest.

- ☐ Marathon's Origin: The myth that the first marathon was run by Pheidippides from the Battle of Marathon to Athens to deliver news of victory is historically dubious.

- ☐ The Football Huddle Curse: Some believe the huddle in football was cursed because it was invented by a deaf player who wanted to hide sign language from opponents.

- ☐ The Football Shape Myth: It's commonly believed that American footballs are called "pigskins" because they were made from pig skin, but they were actually made from cowhide leather.

- ☐ Hockey's Zamboni Curse: A myth in hockey circles suggests that teams who watch the Zamboni ice resurfacer miss their chance to strategize, leading to bad luck.

- ☐ Synchronized Swimming's Nose Clips: The myth that synchronized swimmers wear nose clips to keep water out is only partly true; they also help in maintaining facial expressions underwater.

- ☐ Soccer's Penalty Kick Jinx: Some soccer fans believe that if a player scores on a penalty kick during regular play, they are doomed to miss in a penalty shootout.

- ☐ The Left-Handed Baseball Glove Myth: The myth that left-handed catchers' gloves are bad luck in baseball persists, though it's really about practicality and the rarity of left-handed catchers.

- ☐ The Full Moon Effect in Sports: Some athletes believe a full moon can affect game outcomes, though there's no scientific evidence to support this myth.

Fruits and Vegetables

- ☐ Square Watermelons: In Japan, farmers grow square watermelons by placing them in square glass boxes. They're easier to stack and store, but much more expensive!

- ☐ Carrots Were Originally Purple: The first cultivated carrots weren't orange but purple, along with white and yellow. Orange carrots were developed in the 17th century in the Netherlands.

- ☐ The Exploding Cucumber: The squirting cucumber, when ripe, explosively ejects its seeds and a stream of mucilaginous liquid.

- ☐ Bananas are Berries: Scientifically, bananas are considered berries, while strawberries are not. This is due to their botanical structure and seed arrangement.

- ☐ The Spiciest Pepper: The Carolina Reaper holds the world record for the spiciest pepper, reaching over 2 million units on the Scoville heat scale.

- ☐ Tomatoes Are Fruits... and Vegetables: Botanically, tomatoes are fruits, but in 1893, the U.S. Supreme Court ruled them to be vegetables for taxation purposes.

- ☐ The Seedless Fruit Mystery: Seedless fruits like watermelons and grapes are not genetically modified but are the result of hybridization and special cultivation methods.

- ☐ Grapes and Microwaves: Putting grapes in a microwave can create sparks and even fire due to the concentration of electrolytes in their skins.

- ☐ The 'Vegetable Lamb' Plant: A medieval myth suggested a plant called the Vegetable Lamb of Tartary grew lambs as its fruit.

- ☐ Pineapples Take Years to Grow: It takes about two to three years for a pineapple to grow to its full size.

- ☐ Eggplants Are Berries: Like bananas, eggplants are botanically classified as berries.

- ☐ Oranges Aren't Always Orange: In warmer regions, oranges can remain green even when ripe due to the chlorophyll in their skin.

- ☐ The Fear of Vegetables: Lachanophobia is the fear of vegetables. Yes, it's a real phobia!

- ☐ The World's Heaviest Pumpkin: The heaviest pumpkin ever recorded weighed a staggering 2,624.6 pounds, about the weight of a small car.

- ☐ Apples Float Because They're Airy: Apples are about 25% air, which is why they float in water.

- ☐ Avocados Never Ripen on the Tree: Avocados only start to ripen after they've been picked from the tree.

- ☐ Cucumbers Are 95% Water: This high water content makes them incredibly refreshing, especially in summer.

- ☐ Blueberries Aren't Really Blue: The skin of a blueberry is deep purple, which is why the juice is clear. The blue appearance is due to a natural wax coating.

- ☐ Peppers and Their Gender Myth: Contrary to a popular myth, bell peppers don't have a gender. The number of lobes does not indicate their seed count or sweetness.

☐ The World's Smallest Fruit: The Wolffia globosa, or watermeal, is the world's smallest fruit, about the size of a pinhead.

Foodie Feats

☐ The Largest Pizza: In 2012, Rome, Italy, was home to the creation of the world's largest pizza, named "Ottavia," covering an area of 13,580.28 square feet – the size of two basketball courts!

☐ The Most Expensive Burger: The FleurBurger 5000 in Las Vegas costs $5,000 and includes Wagyu beef, foie gras, truffle, and a bottle of 1995 Château Pétrus.

☐ The Longest Sausage: In 2014, Romania snagged the record for the longest sausage, measuring a whopping 38.99 miles – that's a lot of hot dogs!

☐ The Heaviest Carrot: Grown by a couple in the UK, the heaviest carrot ever recorded weighed 20 pounds – the weight of a small dog.

☐ World's Spiciest Chili: The Carolina Reaper holds the record for the spiciest chili. It's so hot that it's used in pepper spray for self-defense.

☐ The Tallest Cake: In 2008, Indonesia set the record for the tallest cake, standing at 108 feet, about the height of a 10-story building.

☐ The Largest Bowl of Pasta: A bowl of pasta weighing 7,900 kg (about 17,417 pounds) was made in Poland in 2015. That's enough for thousands of servings!

- [ ] The Fastest Time to Eat a Bowl of Pasta: In 2017, Michelle Lesco slurped down a bowl of pasta in just 26.69 seconds.

- [ ] The Most Expensive Ice Cream Sundae: The "Frrrozen Haute Chocolate" sundae, costing $25,000, features edible gold and a side of a gold bracelet at Serendipity 3 in New York City.

- [ ] Giant Gingerbread Houses: In 2013, Texas created a life-size gingerbread house that was not only edible but also large enough to walk into.

- [ ] The Longest Line of Tacos: In 2013, Mexico created the longest line of tacos, stretching for 2,439 meters. That's almost 1.52 miles of tacos!

- [ ] The Largest Chocolate Bar: Weighing in at 12,770 kg (about 28,180 pounds), the largest chocolate bar was made by Thorntons PLC in the UK in 2011.

- [ ] The Most Expensive Cake: In 2015, a cake valued at $75 million was made in the UAE, adorned with diamonds and hand-sculpted fondant.

- [ ] The Fastest Time to Peel and Eat an Orange: The record for peeling and eating an orange is 17.15 seconds, set in 2014.

- [ ] World's Largest Cup of Coffee: In 2019, a cup in South Korea held 14,228.1 liters of coffee – that's enough to keep a whole city awake!

- [ ] The Longest Sandwich: In 2011, Lebanon created a sandwich measuring 735 meters (2,411 feet 5 inches) long. It took hundreds of chefs!

- [ ] The Fastest Time to Eat a 12" Pizza: Kelvin Medina of the Philippines ate a 12" pizza in 23.62 seconds in 2015.

- [ ] The Largest Collection of Cheese Labels: An Italian cheese lover amassed over 32,000 different cheese labels from around the world.

- [ ] The Most Layers in a Sandwich: The most layers in a sandwich is 60, achieved in 2017 – it was almost too tall to bite!

- [ ] The Heaviest Onion: The world's heaviest onion, grown in the UK in 2014, weighed 8.5 kg (about 18.7 pounds) – enough to make anyone cry a river!

Global Food Cultures

- [ ] Italy's Flying Donuts: In Castelnuovo, they have an annual tradition where thousands of donuts are dropped from a helicopter for a festival.

- [ ] Japan's KFC Christmas: Eating KFC on Christmas Eve is a popular tradition in Japan, thanks to a successful marketing campaign in the 1970s.

- [ ] Spain's Tomato Fight: La Tomatina is a festival in Buñol where participants throw thousands of overripe tomatoes at each other – a messy but fun tradition!

- [ ] Sweden's Surströmming: Considered a delicacy, this fermented herring is known for its strong smell and is traditionally eaten outdoors.

- [ ] Norway's Lutefisk Dinner: Made from aged stockfish and lye, lutefisk is a traditional dish typically enjoyed around Christmas.

- [ ] The UK's Cheese Rolling: In Gloucestershire, people chase a rolling cheese wheel down a steep hill. The winner gets the cheese!

- [ ] Iceland's Rotten Shark: Hákarl is a traditional Icelandic dish of fermented Greenland shark, known for its strong ammonia smell and adventurous taste.

- [ ] Germany's Dinner for One: Watching a short British comedy skit called "Dinner for One" is a New Year's Eve tradition in Germany.

- [ ] China's Mooncakes: During the Mid-Autumn Festival, mooncakes are a traditional treat, symbolizing reunion and happiness.

- [ ] India's Thali: A thali is a traditional Indian meal with a variety of dishes served on a single large plate, offering a palette of flavors and textures.

- [ ] Australia's Fairy Bread: A simple treat of bread, butter, and sprinkles, fairy bread is a beloved snack at children's parties in Australia.

- [ ] Korea's Kimjang: The tradition of making and sharing kimchi, called Kimjang, is a way for communities to bond and prepare for winter.

- [ ] Russia's Maslenitsa Pancake Week: Maslenitsa is a week-long celebration in Russia where pancakes are eaten every day to symbolize the sun and the coming of spring.

- [ ] Scotland's Haggis Tossing: Haggis tossing, part of traditional Scottish games, involves throwing a haggis as far as possible for sport.

- [ ] USA's Pie Eating Contests: Pie eating contests, where participants race to eat pies without using their

hands, are a popular and fun event at many
American fairs.

- [ ] Mexico's Day of the Dead Foods: During Día de los
  Muertos, families prepare favorite dishes of
  deceased relatives, including the sweet "pan de
  muerto."

- [ ] Greece's Plate Smashing: Although less common now,
  smashing plates at Greek celebrations is a gesture
  of happiness and good luck.

- [ ] France's Galette des Rois: Eaten in January, this cake
  has a small charm hidden inside. Whoever finds it
  becomes the king or queen for the day.

- [ ] Vietnam's Snake Wine: A traditional beverage where
  a whole snake is steeped in rice wine, believed to
  have medicinal properties.

- [ ] Ethiopia's Coffee Ceremony: Coffee ceremonies are
  an integral part of Ethiopian culture, involving
  roasting, brewing, and serving coffee with great
  hospitality.